Dearest Shelby,

Thank you taking care of Koschka & Mico while we were away. We missed you at the wedding.

Love,
Tamu & Enda

BREAD

and

BUTTER

Ciara McLaughlin is an award-winning designer, cake artist and professional baker living at the foothills of the beautiful Antrim Glens with her parents, siblings and border collie. It was here she grew up surrounded by traditional Irish baking and fell in love with those special moments spent in the kitchen.

A baker by day and creative at heart, she is devoted to passing on an appreciation for homemade food and its place in Irish culture. From her countryside cottage she runs her successful bespoke bakery, Swallow Barn, uniting her passions for art and food through hand-painted treats.

BREAD
and
BUTTER

CAKES AND BAKES FROM GRANNY'S STOVE

CIARA M^CLAUGHLIN

THE O'BRIEN PRESS
DUBLIN

First published 2022 by The O'Brien Press Ltd.,
12 Terenure Road East, Rathgar, Dublin 6, D06 HD27, Ireland.
Tel: +353 1 4923333.
Fax: +353 1 4922777
Email: books@obrien.ie.
Website: obrien.ie
The O'Brien Press is a member of Publishing Ireland.

ISBN 978-1-78849-283-6

10 9 8 7 6 5 4 3 2 1
26 25 24 23 22

Printed by EDELVIVES, Spain.
The paper in this book is produced using pulp from managed forests.

Published in

DUBLIN
UNESCO
City of Literature

CONTENTS

THE STORY

Granny raised her family on an upland farm in County Antrim. Like in most homes in the 1960s, the kitchen was a busy spot, as Granny relied on baking to fill the bellies of her brood of eight, one of which was my daddy. Luckily, in those days culinary competence was woven into her upbringing, so it was no bother meeting the demand for gorgeous grub.

Granny's scullery depended on farm-fresh produce that would make the present organic trend drool. Flavours were dictated by the seasonal crops in Granda's fields or whatever ripe pickings hid in the nearby forest. Putting food on the table was very much a family affair and everyone chipped in – mind you, they didn't have it easy. In the absence of a fridge, perishables were kept outside, clean water had to be laboriously drawn from a well, and the beds were draped with shabby-chic linen, salvaged from flour sacks and stitched by hand. However, these seemingly hard times didn't stop Granny from carving out childhood bliss for Daddy and his siblings, mainly through incredible food.

Fridays at the country haven were forecast for flurries of kitchen bustle, eagerly anticipated by the rising heat in the Rayburn. Wheaten loaves swelled in the oven and the worktops grew heavy with golden pancake medallions, while sodas huddled by the stove. Every so often a turkey wing wiped the flour off the griddle, allowing it to gasp for breath between batches, and there was always someone waltzing with Granny's apron strings in the hope of pinching a wayward crumb.

Granny's family loved her baking, and of course visitors did too. Company would call for a yarn, filling cups from the teapot on the stove and scattering biscuit crumbs from their wagging chins. Any extras were shared with neighbouring houses, delivered by the children for the occasional payment of a pink-powdered bonbon.

Sadly, Granny died before I was born, though I've come to know her through her food. Her baking was thrifty, instinctive and delicious, the kind that nourished and delighted without unnecessary flash. There was nothing artificial about the ingredients she put in or the smiles she got out, and I often find it hard to keep the stories about her baking brief with all the loveliness that crops up. The plates may have been cleared in seconds, but the tastes have lingered on, adopted by my parents when they married. Armed with Daddy's fond memories and Mummy's culinary talents, this dedicated team have preserved Granny's traditions and skills, jotting her recipes in a now exhausted notebook with 'handfuls' and 'drops' translated into measurements.

Naturally, I've grown up with baking as kin, alongside two sisters, a brother and a delightful dog. We've spent many a day crammed in the kitchen, sleeves rolled up and tresses tied back, always ending in the timeless battle to be the licker of the bowl. I'm sure Mummy's head was turned with the four of us teasing her duster with clouds of flour, but she maintained order with the threat of the wooden spoon, which we feared might change from friend to foe.

There's a big difference between Granny's kitchen and ours, but little specks of her history shine through. Every summer since I can remember, Daddy marches us out to the same forest to fill pots and mouths with wild bilberries, and I don't think I'd tasted a store-bought pancake until I was at university (although, I wasn't too impressed). One thing that certainly hasn't changed is the pure appreciation from friends and family upon receiving a box of freshly baked goodies.

It's lovely to think that while Granny worked away by the stove, she was unintentionally piling up a mountainous baking inheritance that has shaped my youth. The past is overflowing with wonderful traditions and flavours, and although it's impractical to fully return to the old ways, a few drops of nostalgia are like a warm, syrupy remedy for the impersonal ache of convenience food. These recipes sing the praises of traditional Irish baking, chiming with the charm of basic, local ingredients and pantry veterans. You can embrace them however you fancy – garnish with a few modish tweaks, mingle with your own family favourites or experiment with vegan alternatives.

This book welcomes baking as an immortal family friend that has sat at the table sharing the craic for generations and captures my appreciation of the glorious moments found between the cupboard and kettle. It's a collection of spectacularly simple recipes that will hopefully inspire you to see the pleasure of making and eating homemade food. It's your basis for traditional, honest baking. It's your Bread and Butter.

INGREDIENTS

Using high quality ingredients is the secret to wonderful baking. In a time before supermarkets, Granny never had to bother with the battle of the brands. Instead, her ingredients came from local crafters and fruits of the season harvested from hedgerows.

FLOUR: Flour is the basis for so many bakes, so it's no wonder that quality flour can make all the difference to the taste of your baked goods. I use Neill's Flour, as I prefer local brands and I can always rely on its high quality, whether I need it to rise or crumble. Neill's Flour may not be available where you are, but look out for your own artisan suppliers. Make sure to note whether the recipe calls for self-raising, plain, strong bread flour or so on, as they all do very different jobs!

EGGS: Free-range eggs are undeniably better for baking, and I find it soothing to know that the hens have a fuller life. For my eggs, I dander down to my neighbouring small business, Green Fingers Family, who are dedicated to nature's welfare and set out an honesty box of the highest quality eggs from their happy hens. Similar homely sellers are popping up all over the countryside, but if supermarkets are your only option, choose free-range eggs for rich, sunny yolks and a little love for the chickens.

SUGAR: This loyal sweetener comes in a plethora of shades and textures. Caster sugar is best for fluffy cakes and light meringues because its fine crystals dissolve quickly. However, in a pinch, I have used standard granulated sugar and so far have had no complaints. Icing sugar is sugar that is ground to a very fine powder, mostly used for buttercream and other icings. Be sure to sift icing sugar to remove any lumps, working slowly and carefully to avoid covering the kitchen! Brown sugar gives bakes a darker colour and a deep sweetness, as it has more molasses. It can be a bit stickier – almost like wet sand – so it's best to crush any lumps through a sieve before mixing into moist cakes and cookies.

BUTTER: With the rise in margarines and low-fat spreads, it's become almost sacred to have 'real butter' in a melty puddle atop toast, and it's also the secret ingredient to exceptional biscuits and buttercream. Blessed by faithful rain, Ireland's pastures are lush and tasty, making happy cows and the richest butter, churned locally by creameries like Dromona in Northern Ireland. For cakes and muffins, I prefer to use margarine to keep them light and moist, but feel free to substitute margarine with butter for a richer flavour.

MILK: There are endless varieties of milk to choose from nowadays. Granny used whole milk for her bakes, delivered daily in glass bottles by the milkman, and she always had a pint of buttermilk in the larder. Made from the leftover liquid once cream has been churned into butter, buttermilk has little to no fat, but it gives a tart creaminess to baked goods while keeping them soft and light. It also has a slightly acidic property that reacts with baking soda to make bread rise, making it essential for plump sodas and wheatens.

BAKING SODA: Also called bicarbonate of soda, this leavening agent is responsible for the bold rise and name of quick breads like soda farls. It's best paired with an acidic liquid like buttermilk, vinegar or lemon juice, as this causes the chemistry that makes for light, fluffy bakes.

BAKING POWDER: A dry white powder to make cakes and buns rise beautifully. Just don't overdo it or it can give an unpleasant bitterness to your baked goods.

FRESH FRUIT AND VEG: Granny's baking followed a seasonal pattern, using produce in its prime. A trip to your local farmers' market can be a fantastic way to gather the freshest local fruits and vegetables, and it's even better if you can grow your own. We grow apples, rhubarb and herbs and forage for wild things like blackberries and bilberries. There is no comparison to the taste of nature's unhurried maturity, and there is something so sweet about the anticipation of the season's harvest.

SPICES: Most kitchens have a spice rack of some sort. Spices work wonders in bringing out the flavour of dishes and conjuring up cosy scents, like the warming fires of ginger or Christmassy cinnamon. Try not to keep those little vessels cooped up in the back of the cupboard too long, though, as the more recently the spice has been ground, the more powerful its aroma.

EQUIPMENT

Part of having an enjoyable, delicious baking experience is making sure that your kitchen is stocked with all the right tools. These don't have to be fancy or expensive (God knows, Granny's weren't) but having a few essential utensils will help you to perform methods properly and make life easier.

SCALES: While Granny's expertise granted her the use of some slapdash measurements, it's best to use scales for reliable, consistent results. Traditional cradle scales look charming on the kitchen worktop but they can make it trickier to be exact. Digital scales give more accurate measurements and are easy to store.

SIEVE: Sifting flour, sugar and icing sugar increases the quality of your bakes by adding air and removing any unwanted lumps. You can also use a sieve to drain excess liquid or remove seeds from cooked fruit.

MIXING BOWL: Mixing bowls are the cauldrons of magic baking memories. Invest in a large, sturdy bowl that will hold hefty mixtures and withstand the brunt of mixing and stirring.

WOODEN SPOON: This is the ultimate kitchen companion for stirring any type of mixture. It's good to have a few different wooden spoons to avoid unwanted flavours mingling – one for general baking, one for savoury sauces and one for jam, which may get stained with the fruity juices.

WHISKS AND MIXERS: A hand-held balloon whisk is a handy tool for quick mixing, but an electric whisk is best for larger mixtures like pancake batter and meringue. To make buttercream, Granny would have softened a block of butter near the fire then creamed it with a wooden spoon until her arm ached, but nowadays stand mixers with a paddle attachment make light work of this labour.

PALETTE KNIFE: Used for giving a smooth, polished finish to all sorts of icings and buttercreams, the palette knife's slick surface is also helpful for sliding biscuits and cookies from their baking trays.

SPATULA: To achieve the satisfaction of a clean bowl, you'll need a good quality silicone spatula. It does a grand job of getting mixture out of every nook and cranny so that you don't waste a drop.

ROLLING PIN: With talents beyond mere rolling out, a rolling pin is a great tool for all kinds of culinary tasks, like gently lifting fondant or pastry and bashing biscuits.

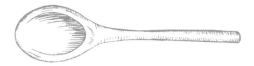

CUTTERS: All sorts of cutters can be used for biscuits, cookies and tarts. It's good to have round cutters in a variety of sizes and ones with scalloped edges to add pretty frills. Novelty cutters are excellent for crafting unique or themed goodies – the possibilities are endless!

BAKING TINS AND TRAYS: Having a variety of tins in different shapes, depths and sizes allows you to master all kinds of bakes. Round tins are perfect for traditional cakes, while loaf tins work well for rustic breads, and a cupcake tin of around 12 holes is a must. A few flat baking trays can be used for biscuits and cookies, with deeper trays used for traybakes and a classic roly-poly sponge (around 9 x 13"/33 x 23cm). Modern features like non-stick coatings and spring-form sides make it much easier to remove the baked goods from the tin.

WIRE RACK: Cooling cakes, biscuits and loaves on a wire rack allows hot air to escape through the bottom to ensure they don't turn soggy. If you're stuck, prop a grill pan on some placemats for a makeshift cooling rack.

BAKING PAPER: Baking paper is incredibly convenient for lining tins and trays to stop baked goods from sticking, and can be made into a lovely rustic wrapper to keep leftovers fresh. Coping without this luxury, Granny used any leftover loaf packaging to wrap her homemade breads (each one used a time or two) and kept her butter papers over a few months to line the tin for the Christmas cake. Thankfully, baking paper is now much more affordable and, for me, it's a kitchen essential.

PASTRY BRUSH: Use a pastry brush for better control when adding egg washes and for less mess when greasing tins.

GRIDDLE OR HEAVY-BASED FRYING PAN: Granny used a griddle pan for much of her baking. It was fashioned from cast iron and heated on the stove to cook soda farls, pancakes and boxty. Nowadays non-stick, plug-in griddles make home baking a simple pleasure, and a heavy-based frying pan set on the hob is a great alternative.

SPRING

The season of spring is effortlessly pleasant, with gentle
showers scattering welly-sized puddles and the first glows of
sun daring to show its face. Nature wakes from its slumber
with a fanfare of daffodils like golden gramophones, buzzing
with the purest optimism for the year that lies ahead. Granny
embraced all of spring's joy through her baking, denoted by
blushing rhubarb and fresh eggs (chocolate ones included,
of course) and guided by important liturgical feasts. These
recipes sing of all the fresh-airiness of the season through
colourful, delicious and traditional spring baking.

CHAMP BOXTY

Boxty exists somewhere between the realms of pancake and rosti, and the variety of potatoey textures shows off the spud as an all-rounder. Granny's recipe uses an emerald fleck of chives, which brings out the provincial flavours of Ulster's well-loved champ.

SERVES 4–6

450g raw potatoes

450g plain flour

1 tsp baking soda

1 tsp salt

2 tbsp chopped chives

450g leftover cooked, mashed potatoes

350ml (approx.) buttermilk

2–3 tsp butter, for frying and serving

- Peel and grate the raw potatoes, then place a small pile onto a square of kitchen paper and lift by the four corners to create a sack around the spuds. Squeeze the kitchen paper over a bowl to extract some of the starchy juice from the potatoes and repeat with the rest of the grated batch.
- Leave the liquid for around 10 minutes, until the starch has settled in a white paste at the bottom of the bowl and separated from the brownish water, then gently pour off the water and stir the starch back into the grated potatoes. This will add crispiness when cooked.
- Place the flour, baking soda, salt and chives in a bowl, then toss in the grated spuds and mix thoroughly with fingertips. Add the mashed potatoes and mix well, then beat in the buttermilk a little at a time until a loose, clumpy batter forms.
- Melt a notch of butter in a frying pan or griddle on medium-high heat. Drop spoonfuls of the mixture into the pan and spread to round, shallow bales. Fry for 4–5 minutes on each side until crisp and golden.
- You can pile the boxty onto a plate in a low oven to stay warm while the rest of the batch cooks, then serve while hot.

A scoop of sour cream with some more chives makes a tasty condiment for a fresh stack.

PANCAKES

Pancakes are champions of both sweet and savoury and can be eaten for pretty much every meal. Granny's recipe is probably a lot healthier than those found on the shelves, due to the tiny amounts of sugar and fat. We make a huge batch on Shrove Tuesday, but their light, fluffy texture ensures that no matter how many times we multiply the mixture, we always want more!

SERVES 4

15g butter

125g self-raising flour

35g sugar

1 egg

300ml milk, or more
  for a thinner batter

- Melt the butter in a saucepan over a low heat. Sift the flour into a bowl, then stir in the sugar and melted butter. Beat the egg separately and pour into the mixture, then gradually whisk in the milk with an electric mixer to form a silky batter. The amount of milk will determine the thickness, so give it a good glug if you want a delicate crepe-like finish or hold back for a chunkier stack.
- Lightly grease a griddle or flat, heavy-based frying pan and set on a medium-high heat. Drop a small ladleful of the mixture onto the griddle pan and then swirl to the desired size. Turn after around 2 minutes, when the heat bubbles burst on the top side, then flip and sizzle on the opposite side for a further 2 minutes.
- While you cook the rest of the batch, keep the pancakes warm by wrapping them in a clean tea-towel.
- Stack the pancakes to serve and top with fresh fruit and a drizzle of maple syrup.

This recipe can be spiced up with loads of fun flavours. Here are some classic combinations.

Raspberry and White Chocolate: Stir 100g frozen raspberries and 50g white chocolate chips into the batter.

Apple and Cinnamon: Finely chop ½ an apple and toss with 1 tbsp brown sugar and 1 tbsp cinnamon, then add to the pancake batter before cooking.

Blueberry: Blueberry pancakes are a breakfast classic, and their juices pack a nutritious punch. Stir a handful carefully into the batter to avoid popping.

Chocolate Chip: Chocolate works with almost everything, including pancakes. Stir 50g chocolate chips into the batter just before cooking.

FRUIT SODA

This oblong loaf may look meek, but a generously buttered slice is a real treat. Granny traditionally indulged in a few slices during Lent, when the family fasted from chocolate and sweets. The rustic loaf has an almost cakey texture, cradled in a gold crust and speckled with the pleasant squishiness of raisins.

SERVES 8–10

400g plain flour

1 tsp baking soda

20g sugar

1 tsp salt

150g raisins or
    sultanas

375ml buttermilk

- Preheat the oven to 220°C/200°C fan/Gas Mark 7 and line a flat baking tray with baking paper.
- Combine the flour, baking soda, sugar, salt and dried fruit in a large baking bowl. Slowly add the buttermilk and mix with a wooden spoon to form a soft, sticky dough.
- Turn the dough out onto a floured surface and pat into an oval loaf. Don't knead the dough, as this will make the bread tough.
- Place the dough onto the baking paper and bake for 15 minutes.
- Reduce the heat to 200°C/180°C fan/Gas Mark 6 and bake for a further 20 minutes. If the loaf is browning too much on top, cover it with baking paper then return to the oven.
- To check if the soda is ready, give its bottom a tap. It will sound hollow when cooked through.

Wrap the loaf in a clean tea-towel while it cools to give it a lovely chewy crust.

POTATO BREAD

Potatoes are undoubtedly the flavour of Irish culture. They were a staple in Granny's kitchen, as she had a plentiful supply from Granda's rigs, but not a bit of spud was wasted, as any leftovers from dinner would be mashed up into earthy slabs of potato bread. Try it fried until crisp with tomato and bacon for a hearty Gaelic brunch on Saint Patrick's Day.

SERVES 4

225g potatoes
½ tsp salt
25g butter
55g self-raising flour

- If you are using leftover cooked potatoes, mash them up with the salt and butter. For raw potatoes, wash, peel and boil until tender, then drain and mash in a large baking bowl. Using the potatoes while still warm will give your bread a lighter texture.
- Use a wooden spoon to work the flour into the mashed potato until it forms a soft dough.
- Tip the dough out onto a lightly floured surface and shape into a round, roughly 1cm thick. Use a sharp knife to cut a cross through the dough, dividing it into 4 equal wedges.
- Heat a griddle or flat, heavy-based frying pan on a medium-high heat.
- Cook the wedges on the hot, dry griddle for 4–5 minutes each side until they develop a toasty giraffe-skin print. They will be quite soft, so handle carefully.
- Allow to cool slightly on a rack then eat while butter-meltingly warm.
- Alternatively, let the potato bread cool completely then enjoy fried or toasted.

Try an avant-garde spud fusion by using sweet potatoes instead. They are naturally sweet and chewy, and will give your plate a bold burst of orange.

Enjoy them toasted the next day, spread with salted butter.

HOT CROSS BUNS

In the run up to Easter, you're sure to find a batch of hot cross buns standing plump and proud, with crosses that are significant of Good Friday. Bursting with sultanas and glazed with honey, they are the perfect blend of sugar and spice and practically insist on being eaten while warm!

MAKES 12

For the buns:
300ml whole milk
50g butter
1 egg
500g strong white
  bread flour
70g caster sugar
1 tsp mixed spice
1 tsp cinnamon
½ tsp ground nutmeg
7g sachet fast-action
  dried yeast
1 tsp salt
200g sultanas
½ tsp sunflower or any
  mildly flavoured oil,
  for greasing

For the cross:
75g flour
2–3 tbsp water

For the glaze:
2 tbsp honey

- Warm the milk over a very low heat, then stir in the butter until melted. Remove the saucepan from the heat and leave to cool slightly. When tepid to the touch, beat in the egg.
- Sift the flour into a large mixing bowl and add the sugar and spices. Place the yeast and salt into the bowl on separate sides then nudge a well into the middle and pour in the butter-egg-milk mixture.
- Stir with a wooden spoon, then use your hands to bring it together to form a soft and sticky dough.
- Turn out the dough onto a lightly floured surface and knead heavily with the heel of your hand for around 5 minutes, until smooth and springy. Knead in the dried fruit until evenly dotted throughout the dough. Lightly oil a clean bowl, then drop the dough in, cover with a damp tea-towel and leave to rise in a warm place until doubled in size, around 1½–2 hours.
- When the bread is risen, give it a punch to get rid of the air, then chop into 12 equal pieces, shaping and tucking each one into a smooth, round bun. Line a flat baking tray with baking paper and arrange the buns onto it, a little apart. Cover with a clean tea-towel and leave on the worktop to prove for about another hour, until they rise up and nestle into one another.
- Preheat the oven to 220°C/200°C fan/Gas Mark 7. Meanwhile, mix the flour with water, 1 tbsp at a time, to make a thick paste. Use a piping bag with a fine-tipped nozzle to give each bun a neat little cross.
- Bake for 15–20 minutes, until swollen with a golden glow.
- While warm, brush with a lick of honey to add sweetness and shine, then transfer to a wire rack to cool.

Cakes & Buns

YOGHURT LOAF CAKE

Breezy spring days are a tonic for winter-induced cabin fever. The dry winds seem to lure every stitch to the washing line for a breath of fresh air, and boundless chores are uncovered. Baking a yoghurt loaf cake is an appealing task for the to-do list, as the novelty of the yoghurt-pot measurements is great fun and keeps dishes to a minimum, so you can get on with the spring-cleaning!

SERVES 8–10

Use the same yoghurt pot for the measurements throughout.

3 eggs
1 pot any yoghurt of a
   pourable consistency
   (about 150g for
   a 2lb/900g loaf)
1 pot corn oil, or any
   mildly flavoured oil
3 pots self-raising flour
1 pot caster sugar

- Preheat the oven to 190°C/170°C/Gas Mark 5 and grease and line a 2lb/900g loaf tin.
- Crack the eggs into a bowl then pour in the yoghurt and oil and whisk to combine.
- Wash and dry the yoghurt pot and use it to measure 3 pots of flour, then sift the flour into a separate large baking bowl and stir in 1 pot of sugar. Nudge a deep well into the centre of the dry ingredients and pour in the liquid, then mix with a wooden spoon or spatula until fully combined into a smooth batter. Pour the batter into the loaf tin.
- Bake for 45–50 minutes until well risen and a skewer placed in the centre comes out without crumbs.
- Set aside to cool for a few moments, then tip the cake from the tin and place on a wire rack. When the loaf cake is cool, slice thickly to serve.

Vary the flavour
of yoghurt – try
strawberry or honey
for a subtle tang.

BUTTERFLY BUNS

In the days before elaborate foil-wrapped bunnies and chicks, Granny's Easter spread relied on the humble genius of the butterfly bun. These fluffy buns are easy to make but brighten the table with an adorable flutteriness. A novelty for kids and nostalgic for adults – it's no wonder they're a bake-sale favourite!

MAKES 12

For the buns:

100g margarine

100g caster sugar

2 eggs

125g self-raising flour

For the topping:

50g butter, room
   temperature

100g icing sugar

½ tsp vanilla extract

6 tsp strawberry jam,
   for decorating

- Preheat the oven to 190°C/170°C fan/Gas Mark 5 and line a 12-hole baking tin with bun cases.
- Cream the margarine and sugar with an electric mixer until pale and fluffy. Crack the eggs into a separate bowl to make sure they are free of any discoloured flecks or shards of shell, then beat into the mixture until smooth. Sift the flour and fold into the mixture using a wooden spoon or spatula to form a creamy batter. Scoop the batter evenly into the bun cases.
- Bake for 15–20 minutes, until risen with a deep tan.
- Remove from the tin and leave to cool on a wire rack, then slice the tops off the buns and cut each top in two to form wings.
- To make the topping, cream the butter until soft and whippy. Sift in the icing sugar a little at a time and beat slowly to avoid sugary puffs escaping. Add the vanilla and continue to beat until smooth and pale.
- Dollop a little buttercream on top of each bun and arrange the wings in place, then blob on half a teaspoon of jam for the abdomen.

For classic cupcakes, leave the buns whole and pipe the buttercream in a neat swirl on top. You can also brighten up the buttercream with a few drops of food colouring and sprinkles.

LEMON DRIZZLE CAKE

Spring needs the bright lift of lemon to shake off the winter dregs. Its colour mirrors the yellow daffodils popping out in clusters amidst grey skies, promising the growth of the season to come. With a light, tangy taste and flecks of brilliant gold, this loaf cake sings of sunnier days and vivid floral fields.

SERVES 8–10

For the cake:
250g butter, softened
250g caster sugar
4 eggs
250g self-raising flour
3 unwaxed lemons,
    zest only

For the icing:
100g icing sugar
3 unwaxed lemons,
    juice only

- Preheat the oven to 160°C/140°C fan/Gas Mark 3 and line a 2lb/900g loaf tin with baking paper.
- Cream the butter and sugar with an electric mixer until pale and fluffy, then beat in eggs until well combined. Sift in the flour, then finely grate in the lemon zest and fold to a thick batter, dispersing any pockets of flour. Save the juice of the lemons for the icing later.
- Pour the mixture into the prepared loaf tin and even out the top with the back of a spoon.
- Bake for 45–50 minutes, until a skewer in the centre comes out cake-free. When baked, transfer the cake to a wire rack and stab all over with the skewer to make veins for the drizzle to soak through.
- Sift the icing sugar into a bowl and gradually add the juice from the lemons one tablespoon at a time until the icing can be easily poured.
- Spoon the drizzle over the cake while it still holds a slight warmth, as the heat will help it drink up the zestiness.

Using fresh, free-range eggs helps give the cake a daffodilly glow.

Colour the marzipan by
adding edible colour dust
or paste to compliment
the crystallised flora.

SIMNEL CAKE

Historically, simnel cake was baked on Mothering Sunday to celebrate the one day a year that servant girls were permitted to visit home. It's now more commonly associated with Easter and, with its sunny yellow marzipan topped with sugar-coated petals, it heralds the springtime celebration.

SERVES 10–12

For the sugared flowers:
Handful of edible flowers
    (primroses, pansies, etc.)
1 large egg white
1 tsp water
1 tbsp caster sugar

For the marzipan:
550g shop-bought
    marzipan
or
250g caster sugar
250g ground almonds
1 tsp almond extract
2 eggs

For the cake:
175g butter, softened
175g caster sugar
3 eggs
2 tbsp milk
225g self-raising flour,
    plus extra for dusting
2 tsp cinnamon
1 tsp nutmeg
250g raisins
200g sultanas
75g mixed peel
2 tbsp apricot jam

- Prepare the sugared flowers the day before by lightly mixing the egg white with water, then brushing onto the petals. Sprinkle liberally with caster sugar and leave to dry out overnight.
- For the marzipan, stir together the sugar, ground almonds and almond extract. Beat the eggs separately, then gradually mix into the bowl to make a soft paste. On a lightly floured surface, knead the marzipan until smooth, then roll out one-third and use a 7 inch/18cm cake tin to cut out a round to fit. Wrap the remaining marzipan in baking paper and reserve for later.
- Preheat the oven to 170°C/150°C fan/Gas Mark 3 and lightly grease the 7 inch/18cm round cake tin.
- To make the cake, cream the butter and sugar with an electric mixer until light and fluffy, then beat in the eggs and milk. Sift in the flour and spices and stir until smooth. In a separate bowl, dust the dried fruits and mixed peel with a little flour to stop them from sinking, then fold into the mixture.
- Pour half of the mixture into the tin, then cover with the marzipan disc. Spoon in the remaining mixture and smooth with a palette knife.
- Bake for 55–60 minutes, then lower the heat to 150°C/130°C fan/Gas Mark 2 and bake for a further 2 hours. Remove the cake from the oven and leave in the tin to cool slightly. After around 20 minutes, slide the cake out onto a wire rack to cool completely.
- Roll out half the remaining marzipan and, again, use the cake tin to cut a 7 inch/18cm round, pressing your thumb around the edge for a frilly finish.
- Slather apricot jam on top of the fruit cake to act as glue for the marzipan round, then use the remaining marzipan to roll 11 little balls. Traditionally, these represent the 11 apostles of Jesus, after Judas' infamous betrayal.
- Brush the bottom of each mini-apostle with water and dot around the fringes of the cake, then embellish with the sugared flowers.

JAM TARTS

Making homemade jam tarts is a ludicrously simple process, using easy-peasy steps and the most basic of ingredients. But here these humble kitchen must-haves are transformed into lavish tarts, with rich buttery cases and glossy pools of crimson that are so good they're fit for a queen!

MAKES 12

100g butter
200g plain flour
3–4 tbsp cold water
12 tsp strawberry jam

- Preheat the oven to 200°C/180°C fan/Gas Mark 6.
- In a large bowl combine the butter and flour by rubbing with light fingertips to form crumbs. Drop in the water one tablespoonful at a time and mix with a knife to form a dough. You can use your hands to bring the dough together at the end, but try to avoid over-kneading.
- Wrap the dough snugly in baking paper and leave to chill in the fridge for 15 minutes.
- Roll the dough out on a lightly floured surface to about 3mm thickness, then use a round cutter to make discs big enough to line each hole of a 12-hole shallow bun tin. I like to use a cutter with crinkly edges for pretty frills. Plop one heaped teaspoon of jam into each pastry case, leaving it just shy of the top, as overfilling can be messy.
- Bake for 12–15 minutes until the rims are golden and the jammy lava is bubbling lightly.
- Remove from the oven and allow to cool for a few minutes in the tin before carefully transferring the tarts to a wire rack to cool completely.

Strawberry jam will give a traditional look, but you can mix up the colours to make a medley of jammy jewels.

MELTING
CHOCOLATE HEARTS

Valentine's Day can be cloying for some. Nevertheless, it's a special time to treat the ones you love and a great excuse to indulge in the most romantic of ingredients: chocolate! These cocoa-filled nuggets melt dreamingly on your tongue and suit any state of heart.

MAKES 12

For the biscuits:
175g butter, softened
75g icing sugar
1 tsp vanilla extract
150g plain flour
25g cornflour
25g cocoa powder

For the filling:
100g dark chocolate
100g butter
60g icing sugar

- For the biscuits, beat the butter, icing sugar and vanilla extract together with an electric mixer until smooth and creamy. Sift the flour, cornflour and cocoa powder to remove any lumps, then stir into the mixture with a spoon or spatula until a soft, tawny dough is formed. Wrap the dough in baking paper and chill in the fridge for around 1 hour until firm.
- Preheat the oven to 180°C/160°C fan/Gas Mark 4 and line two flat baking trays with baking paper.
- Roll the dough out to about ½cm thick, then cut out 24 heart shapes and arrange on the baking tray, allowing a little space between each.
- Bake for 10–12 minutes, until the biscuit rims begin to darken, then remove from the oven and leave to firm up slightly before transferring to a wire rack to cool.
- To make the filling, melt the chocolate in a bowl over a pot of simmering water, or carefully in the microwave, then leave aside to cool until it is no longer hot to the touch. In a separate bowl, cream the butter and sugar with an electric mixer until light in colour, then pour in the melted, cooled chocolate and beat briskly.
- Use a piping bag to swirl chocolate buttercream onto the flat side of one biscuit then place a partner on top to finish the chocolate sandwich.

Sharp, fruity flavours work fantastically in place of the chocolate filling. Stew and strain 65g raspberries and add to the creamed butter and sugar with a few drops of pink food colouring for a tinge of amour.

CUSTARD CREAMS

For years, custard creams have held a customary position on the biscuit plate. There's nothing too glamorous about them, but they are sensational with a cup of tea, and homemade ones always taste best. These crunchy biccies hold a silky vanilla filling, and their pretty petalled shapes echo the innocent pleasure of plucking daisies from the garden to make nature's bling.

MAKES 12

For the biscuits:
115g butter, softened
55g icing sugar
1½ tbsp milk
1 tsp vanilla extract
170g plain flour
60g custard powder

For the filling:
75g butter, softened
150g icing sugar
2 tsp vanilla extract
1 tbsp custard powder

- Preheat the oven to 180°C/160°C fan/Gas Mark 4 and line two flat baking trays with baking paper.
- To make the biscuits, beat the butter and sugar until pale and fluffy using an electric mixer, then pour in the milk and vanilla and mix until creamy. Sift in the flour along with the custard powder and bring together by hand to a soft dough. Use a light touch and avoid over-handling the dough for that melt-in-the-mouth texture.
- Wrap the dough in a layer of baking paper and set in the fridge for about 20 minutes or so to chill.
- Turn the dough out onto a lightly floured surface and roll to around ½cm thick. Use a flower-shaped cookie cutter to make 24 rounds, and transfer to the baking tray, leaving a little space around each, then use a small round cutter to cut a little centre circle out of half of the batch.
- Bake for 8–10 minutes until the edges turn pale gold. Remove from the oven, allow the biscuits to firm up a little, then carefully transfer to a wire rack to cool.
- To make the filling, beat the butter and icing sugar together with a wooden spoon or electric mixer until pale and smooth, then drop in the vanilla and custard powder and continue mixing until combined.
- When the biscuits have cooled, pipe a splodge of creamy custard onto the underside of the whole ones, then sandwich with the remaining biscuits and serve with a cuppa.

Add a few drops of food colouring to the custard buttercream filling for pretty coloured centres.

CHOCOLATE NESTS

After a childhood spent rummaging in the hedgerows, Daddy is now the ultimate bird expert.
Many a spring morning he spent ducked in mossy ditches, hopefully awaiting a glimpse of a
brooding chaffinch or wren fledglings, and he knows a thing or two about building nests – even
ones made of chocolate!

MAKES 12

200g milk chocolate
90g shredded wheat
1 packet mini sugar eggs
(the really mini ones
are the most realistic)

- Line a 12-hole baking tin with bun cases.
- Melt the chocolate in a heatproof bowl over a pan of simmering water or carefully in the microwave.
- In another bowl, bash the pillows of shredded wheat lightly with a rolling pin until broken, but not crushed.
- Tip the scraggly strands into the melted chocolate and stir with a metal spoon until fully coated.
- Spoon a few heaped teaspoons of the mixture into each bun case and press a small dip in the centre to make the nest. Avoid being overly neat, as you want to give a rugged, built-by-the-beak appearance.
- Pop a few tiny sugar eggs into each nest to finish the brood.

Keeping the eggs the
same colour in each
nest will make them
look more convincing.

JAM SANDWICH BISCUITS

These biccies are reminiscent of the oozing jam sandwiches that were a staple part of Granny's picnic lunches. Their little love-heart windows flaunt gooey ruby centres, giving them a lovey-dovey look that is perfect for Valentine's Day.

MAKES 16

225g butter, softened

125g icing sugar, plus extra for dusting

1 tsp vanilla extract

2 egg yolks

320g plain flour

6 tbsp seedless strawberry jam (or regular jam, sieved to remove seeds)

- Use an electric mixer to beat the butter and icing sugar until pale and soft. Beat in the vanilla and egg yolks until fully combined. Sift in the flour and stir with a wooden spoon until a soft dough is formed.
- Wrap the dough in baking paper and place in the fridge for around 1 hour until firm.
- Preheat the oven to 180°C/160°C fan/Gas Mark 4 and line two flat baking trays with baking paper.
- Roll out the dough onto a lightly floured surface to around ½cm thick. The dough will be quite soft so needs only a light touch. Use a medium-sized cutter to stamp out 32 circles, then place the biscuits evenly onto the baking trays, allowing a little space between each. When the biscuits are on the tray, use a small heart-shaped cutter to cut romantic little peep-holes in half of the batch. It's best to do this when the biscuits are on the tray so the hearts don't get squashed out of shape. (You can roll the heart cut-outs together into dough for more jam biscuits or bake them as plain mini hearts.)
- Bake the biscuits for 10–12 minutes, until their fringes turn light gold.
- Remove from the oven and allow to rest on the tray for a minute or so to firm up, then lift onto a wire rack to cool.
- When completely cool, sprinkle the tops with icing sugar. Spread a splodge of jam onto the whole biscuit bases, then crown with the dusted window biscuits.

Play with the theme by using an assortment of cutters like stars or circles for the middles.

When piping the biscuits,
use a cocktail stick to
pop any small air bubbles
and to nudge the icing
out to the edges.

EASTER BISCUITS

Pastel-painted biscuits are an emblem of Easter. Each bite crumbles with a light, buttery crunch, and their sugar-coated shades of pink, green and lilac brandish the prettiness of the season. Cut them into shapes of chicks, bunnies and eggs for dainty and delicious spring treats.

MAKES 16–20

For the biscuits:
150g butter, softened
90g caster sugar
280g plain flour
½ tsp baking soda
1 tsp ground cinnamon
½ tsp ground ginger
A pinch of salt

For the royal icing, choose one of the recipes below and follow the same method:

Instant powder:
35ml cold water
225g royal icing powder

Powdered egg-white:
45ml water
250g icing sugar
8g egg-white powder

Raw egg-white:
1 egg white
225g icing sugar

Variety of food colouring

- Preheat the oven to 180°C/160°C fan/Gas Mark 4, and line a flat baking tray with baking paper.
- Beat the butter and sugar with an electric mixer until pale and fluffy.
- Sift the flour, baking soda, spices and salt into the mixture and mix with a wooden spoon, then use your hands to knead together into a soft dough.
- On a lightly floured surface, roll the dough to about ½cm thick. From the dough canvas, use cookie cutters to cut chicks, bunnies, eggs or any other tokens of spring you like, and place on the baking tray, leaving a little room between each one. Use a second lined tray if needed.
- Place the baking tray into the fridge to chill the dough for 10 minutes. This will stop the biscuits spreading in the oven and preserve their shape.
- Bake for 12–15 minutes until the edges turn pale gold. Remove from the oven and leave the biscuits on the tray for a minute or so to firm up, then carefully transfer to a wire rack to cool.
- To decorate, place the liquid (water or egg white, depending on your choice of recipe) into a bowl and add half of the icing sugar or royal icing powder. Start mixing slowly to avoid losing puffs of the powder. When combined, add the remaining powders and continue to beat to a thick, glossy icing (you can add more water a few drops at a time if the icing looks too stiff). Separate the icing into different bowls and add a few drops of food colouring to tint each batch. Pastel shades work nicely for a spring palette.
- Transfer the icing to a piping bag with a thin nozzle and carefully squeeze onto each biscuit, starting at the edges and working towards the centre.
- Leave the biscuits flat for at least 4 hours, or preferably overnight, for the icing to fully set, then store in an airtight container for 3–4 days.

APPLE RICE PUDDING

This was Granny's staple dessert. After dotting individual pots with stewed apples, she would ladle the rice on top and leave the batch by the open window to cool in the breeze. That is until one day the cat snuck in the window to cruelly take a click from each pot! Sadly, there was no dessert that night, and the cat was persona non grata for a day or two.

SERVES 4

For the apples:
500g cooking apples
50g sugar

For the rice:
100g pudding rice
1 litre milk
1 tbsp sugar
1 tsp cinnamon,
  for dusting

- Peel, quarter and chunk the apples, then add to a heavy-based saucepan and sprinkle in the sugar. Cook over a medium heat for 10–15 minutes, until they stew to a soft appley slush. Dollop the stewed fruit into the bottom of 4 individual bowls or jars and set aside to cool.
- Add the rice, milk and sugar to a heavy-based saucepan.
- Bring the contents to a boil then reduce the heat to a simmer and stir continuously to avoid patches sticking to the bottom.
- Continue cooking the rice on the hob for a further 30 minutes, stirring constantly until it is thick and soft to bite.
- Top each bowl of stewed apples with a snowy mound of rice pudding and finish with a light dusting of cinnamon.

Swap stewed apples for any fruit of preference, or top the rice pudding with a few spoonfuls of jam.

PAVLOVA

After dandering through byways laced with cow-parsley cuffs, it's no wonder Granny had a notion for something delicate and fresh – just like this silky pavlova. The ivory dessert has a crisp shell, a mallowy inner chew and an abundant heap of fruit on top to celebrate the pop of spring colours.

SERVES 8–10

For the meringue:
6 egg whites
350g caster sugar
1 tsp vanilla extract
1 tsp white vinegar
2 tsp cornflour

For the decoration:
250ml double cream
Fresh fruit of your
    choice

- Preheat the oven to 170°C/150°C fan/Gas Mark 3.
- Use a dinner plate or cake tin to draw a 10 inch/25cm circle on a sheet of baking paper and use it to line a baking tray.
- Crack the eggs and separate the whites from the yolks. The yolks can be stored in the fridge for up to 2 days and used in custards, curds or other recipes (try the Jam Sandwich Biscuits on page 44 or Chocolate Caramel Fondants on page 138). Use an electric mixer to whip the egg whites until foamy, then gradually whisk in the sugar to form lustrous snowy peaks. If you can hold the bowl over your head without being dripped on, they are ready!
- Whisk in the vanilla extract, vinegar and cornflour. Use the circle on the baking paper as a guide for spreading the mixture into a swirly round.
- Bake for 1 hour, or until the white shell looks dry and firm. Don't be tempted to open the oven during this time, as this could make the pavlova flop. Turn off the heat but keep the pavlova inside the oven for at least a couple of hours, or preferably overnight, until it has fully cooled to prevent it from cracking too much.
- Just before serving, whip the double cream until thick, light and airy.
- Decorate the pavlova with a layer of whipped cream and top with segments of fruit.

For a healthier topping, substitute the cream with crème fraiche or yoghurt.

If individual tarts seem too
fiddly, make the custard tart
in one large dish and serve in
slices. You may need to add
5–10 minutes to the baking
times to let the middle cook.

EGG-CUSTARD TARTS

Hens were hugely important patrons of Granny's kitchen, and each morning a sleepy-eyed collector was sent to snatch half a dozen eggs from the straw. The chore risked a run-in with an aggrieved Banty hen, but the we'ans went armed with pocketfuls of meal to tempt the feathered guards from their nests. Having chickens is a great way to keep the kitchen stocked, but if you're buying eggs, look for free range or organic.

MAKES 12

For the pastry:
200g plain flour
Pinch of salt
100g butter,
   chilled and cut
   into small cubes
3–4 tbsp water

For the filling:
600ml milk
1 tsp vanilla extract
4 egg yolks
4 tbsp sugar
2 tsp ground nutmeg

- Preheat the oven to 220°C/200°C fan/Gas Mark 7. Cut 12 strips of baking paper and lay one inside each hole of a 12-hole shallow bun tin with a little overhang at either side. This will allow you to hoist each tart from the tin without cracking the pastry.
- To make the pastry, sift the flour and salt into a baking bowl, then rub in the butter to make fine breadcrumbs. Sprinkle in the water and stir with a knife until it begins to bind together.
- Bring together by hand, giving a brief, gentle knead to make a firm dough. Wrap the dough in baking paper and chill in the fridge for 20 minutes or so.
- Roll the dough out onto a lightly floured surface to about 3mm thickness, turning it occasionally to stop it sticking. Cut 12 rounds from the dough, a bit bigger than the diameter of the holes in the tin, and gently press one round into each hole.
- To make the custard, warm the milk and vanilla over a low heat.
- In a separate bowl, use an electric mixer to whisk the egg yolks and sugar together until pale and smooth, then continue to whisk as you pour in the warm vanilla-milk. Strain the custard through a sieve into a measuring jug, then flood each pastry case as high as possible without overspills and sprinkle with nutmeg.
- Bake for 8–10 minutes, until the pastry edges begin to brown, then reduce the oven temperature to 180°C/160°C fan/Gas Mark 4 and bake for a further 10–15 minutes, until the custard has the slightest dome. Don't worry if the middles are still jiggly as they will set when cooled.
- Leave in the tin for 30 minutes or so, then use the baking paper hammocks to raise each tart from the tin and set on a wire rack to cool completely before devouring.

RHUBARB CRUMBLE

With its slender crimson legs and flouncy green skirts, it's no wonder rhubarb is making a comeback in vogue cuisine. Granny loved it because it's cheap and hardy, and there's now a rising obsession with its vintage tang. Part of its beauty is its ability to flourish in cooler conditions with minimal fuss, but if it's not practical for you to grow and gather fresh rhubarb, you can buy it in the shops from early spring.

SERVES 6–8

For the filling:
500g rhubarb
100g sugar (adjust
    to taste depending
    on the sweetness
    of the rhubarb)
2 tbsp water

For the crumble:
225g flour
115g butter
150g sugar

- Preheat the oven to 190°C/170°C fan/Gas Mark 5.
- Wash and chop the rhubarb stalks into chunks (about 2cm), then place in a saucepan with the sugar and water. Stew over a medium heat for 15 minutes to a ruby mush, then decant into an oven-proof dish.
- To make the crumble, rub the flour and butter together, lifting and dropping the mixture lightly through your fingertips until it resembles breadcrumbs, then use a wooden spoon to stir in the sugar.
- Tip the golden sand over the stewed fruit and give the dish a gentle shake to ensure an even spread.
- Bake for 35–40 minutes, until the crumble starts to lightly brown and the jammy juices lap around the edges.
- Slice the crumble into sizeable segments and serve with the classic spouse of custard.

Make the crumble
healthier by swapping half
the sugar for desiccated
coconut or oats.

LEMON MERINGUE PIE

Granny's lemon meringue pie is the ideal dessert for a spring afternoon. Its lemon curd filling is deliciously light, topped with scrunches of toasty meringue. A perfect balance of squashy, crisp, sweet and tart, this traditional dessert is sure to satisfy every guest.

SERVES 6–8

For the pastry:

175g plain flour

100g butter

1 tbsp icing sugar

1 egg

For the filling:

150ml cold water

75g caster sugar

3 tbsp cornflour

2 large lemons

25g butter

2 large egg yolks

For the topping:

2 large egg whites

1 tbsp cornflour

100g caster sugar

- Preheat the oven to 200°C/180°C/Gas Mark 6 and lightly grease an 8 inch/20cm loose-bottomed fluted tin.
- To make the pastry, rub the butter and flour with light fingertips to form crumbs, then stir in the icing sugar. Beat the egg, then pour into the dry ingredients and bring together by hand. Wrap the dough in baking paper and chill in the fridge for around 20 minutes.
- Roll the dough out onto a lightly floured surface to a couple of centimetres wider than the diameter of the tin, then use the rolling pin to drape it over the tin. Press it gently into the bottom and sides, then trim any excess with a blunt knife and prick the bottom sporadically with a fork.
- Line the base and sides with a circle of baking paper, then tip in some dried peas and place the tin on a tray.
- Bake for 15 minutes, then remove the paper and dried peas and bake for 5 minutes more until pale gold. Remove from the oven and leave in the tin to cool. Reduce the oven temperature to 180°C/160°C fan/Gas Mark 4.
- For the filling, combine the water, sugar and cornflour in a saucepan, then add the zest and juice of the lemons. Bring to the boil, then reduce to a simmer, stirring constantly until thick. Remove from the heat and stir in the butter until melted. Let the mixture cool slightly, then beat in the egg yolks until smooth and pour into the pastry case.
- Whisk the egg whites with an electric mixer until stiff (see tip), then whisk in the cornflour and caster sugar, one spoonful at a time, until glossy and thick. Dollop the meringue on top of the pie, using the back of a spoon to make a swooping peaked texture.
- Bake for 35–40 minutes until the swirls of meringue slightly singe.
- Remove from the oven and leave in the tin for around 30 minutes to cool, then gently press from the bottom to release the pie from the fluted sides.
- Chill the pie in the fridge for at least an hour before slicing to serve.

When making the
meringue, make sure
your bowl is completely
dry, otherwise the egg
whites won't stiffen.

SUMMER

Late sunsets are a summertime treasure, but on Granda's
farm a stretch in the evenings meant longer labour. Good
job Granny was there to keep spirits high with picnic baskets
of fresh bread, jam and lemonade, spread on a blanket in
the glades. She spent hazy afternoons plucking juice-filled
baubles of berries from the bushes and treating her children
to tasty 'school's-out' snacks. These recipes are perfect for
picnics and parties, mopping up the bursts of seasonal fruits
to bring summery shades to the table.

Breads

BELFAST BAPS

It's no wonder Ireland has legends of giants when you see the enormous serving of a Belfast bap!
There's some eating in one of these chunks of delicious fresh bread, charred with a crusty top and
doused with plenty of flour. Load one up with your favourite fillings and it'll keep you going all day.

MAKES 6

2 x 7g sachets fast-
    action dried yeast
½ tsp sugar
625ml tepid water
885g strong white
    bread flour
½ tsp salt
A little rice flour
    or semolina
    for dusting

- Pour the yeast and sugar into a baking bowl and add the tepid water (about the temperature of your hand), then leave for 8–10 minutes until frothy.
- Sift the flour into the yeasty foam then add the salt, mixing until a smooth dough forms. You might need to add a little extra flour to bring the dough to a point where it is pulling away cleanly from the sides of the bowl.
- Tip the dough out onto a lightly floured surface and knead with the heel of your hand for 8–10 minutes until springy and elastic. Lightly oil a bowl, pop the dough inside and cover with a damp tea-towel.
- Leave in a warm place to prove for 1½–2 hours until doubled in size.
- When risen, punch the air out of the dough and tip out onto a surface sprinkled with rice flour or semolina. Divide the dough into 6 equal pieces, shaping each segment into a ball, then place closely, but not touching, on a lined baking tray and douse with a thick sprinkling of rice flour. Loosely drape a damp tea-towel over and leave to prove again for a further 45 minutes.
- Preheat the oven to 200°C/180°C fan/Gas Mark 6.
- When hot, place a tray of boiling water in the bottom of the oven as the bread goes in to create steam.
- Bake for 30 minutes, then turn up the heat to 240°C/220°C fan/Gas Mark 9 and continue to cook for a further 5–10 minutes until the top starts blackening. Don't fear a dark crust as it is desirable for traditional Belfast baps to have a little charred crackling on top.
- Remove from the oven and slide onto a wire rack to cool.

For a true taste of Ireland, fill a bap with a packet of Tayto crisps and dig in!

MUMMY'S FAMOUS SCONES

Scones were Granny's bank holiday treat, baked fresh that morning and topped with lavish cream caps. Mummy has since perfected the recipe into legendary status, and they are always baked for guests, cautiously served on the good china with a dollop of cream and homemade jam. Bake a batch to impress friends and family but be prepared to receive lots of recipe requests!

MAKES 16

600g self-raising flour
100g margarine
4 tsp sugar
1 egg
Around 400ml milk

- Preheat the oven to 220°C/200°C fan/Gas Mark 7.
- Rub the flour and margarine together with your fingertips, then add the sugar to the rubble mixture. Beat the egg in a measuring jug, then pour in enough milk to reach 450ml. Add this yolky cocktail to the baking bowl and mix everything with a metal knife until a dough forms. It should be sticky, as this will give the scones a light fluffiness.
- Put your hands into the squelchy goo and cradle it out onto a floured surface, being as gentle as possible to avoid stamping the air out of the dough. Lightly pat to a thick slab of around 2cm thick, then cut out the scones with a circular cutter and place on a baking tray.
- Bake in the oven for 10–12 minutes, until proudly risen and just bronzing on top. Pile onto a plate and serve with a splodge of jam and cream.

Scones are a great base for experimenting with different flavours. Here are some combinations:

Raspberry and White Chocolate: Gently stir in 100g frozen raspberries and 50g white chocolate chips before adding the wet ingredients.

Apple and Cinnamon: Roll the dough into a long rectangle, about 1cm thick. Sprinkle with cinnamon and one small apple, finely chopped. Roll up the dough, starting at the long side, then slice into 14–16 spirals and bake as above.

Date and Wheaten: Replace half of the self-raising flour with wholewheat flour and 1 tsp baking soda. Mix in 50g chopped dates, before adding the wet ingredients.

Lemon and Coconut: Roll the dough into a long rectangle, about 1cm thick, and spread on a layer of lemon curd (page 194) and sprinkle with coconut. Roll up the dough, starting at the long side, then slice into 14–16 spirals and bake as above.

Granny limited her children
to butter or jam, but you
can break this rule.

BATCH LOAF

Making bread may seem daunting, but Granny's recipe had to be simple so that batches could be baked daily to save a five-mile trip to the local shop. Naturally, it's now become the norm to buy a loaf, but the seductive scent of a dough-filled oven might give you an appetite for baking your own. This recipe makes four loaves together in one tin, giving the traditional torn sides and crusty top.

MAKES 4

450ml tepid water

10g fast-action dried
    yeast (1½ sachets)

650g strong white
    bread flour, plus
    extra for dusting

10g salt

35g vegetable oil

- Place half of the tepid water (about the temperature of your hand) into a small bowl and add the yeast. Stir the liquid and leave to settle for 8–10 minutes to allow the yeast to activate.
- Sift the flour into a large baking bowl and stir in the salt and oil. Pour the yeast liquid into the bowl then gradually add the remaining water, mixing well until a smooth dough forms. You might need a little more or less water to bring the dough to a consistency where it just has the slightest stickiness.
- Tip the dough out onto a lightly floured surface and use the heel of your hand to knead for at least 8 minutes, until silky and elastic. Alternatively, use a mixer with a dough hook. Lightly oil a bowl, then drop the dough into the bowl and cover with a damp tea-towel. Leave in a warm place to rise for 1½–2 hours, until doubled in size.
- When the bread has risen, give it a punch to knock the air out, then divide into four equal pieces and form each into a ball.
- Line an 8 inch/20cm square deep tin with baking paper. Set the dough balls in the bread tin, close together so they can join snugly in the oven.
- Sprinkle their tops with a decent pinch of flour, then cover with a tea-towel and leave on the worktop to rise again for around 45 minutes.
- Preheat the oven to 260°C/240°C fan/Gas Mark 10. When the oven is hot, fill a separate tray with boiling water and place in the oven as the bread goes in to make steam that will give the bread a nice crust on top.
- Bake for 35 minutes, then turn down the heat to 200°C/180°C fan/Gas Mark 6 and bake for a further 10 minutes, until the tops are dark and crisp and the bottoms sound hollow when tapped.
- Remove from the oven, slide the loaves from the tin and place on a wire rack to cool. When ready to use, tear the bread into individual loaves and cut into ridiculously thick slices.

LEMON CURD FLATBREAD

The amber glow of this flatbread is like sunshine on a plate, and it's the perfect canvas to show off Granny's lemon curd. This is our go-to BBQ dessert, cooked al fresco on a hot stone and topped with a sprig of mint.

SERVES 6–8

For the base:

¼ tsp fast-action dried yeast

80ml water (tepid if using the dough the same day, cold if using the next)

125g strong white bread flour

1 tsp extra virgin olive oil

Pinch of salt

For the topping:

2–4 tbsp lemon curd (page 194)

10g desiccated coconut

2 tsp icing sugar

6–8 mint leaves

- To make the base, mix the yeast and water in a bowl until dissolved and allow to stand for 8–10 minutes.
- Sift the flour into a large baking bowl then stir in the olive oil and salt. When the yeast solution turns cloudy, add it to the baking bowl and mix with a wooden spoon to form a dough.
- Tip the dough out onto a lightly floured surface and knead for around 10 minutes, until it is smooth and springs back when prodded.
- Place the dough in a large, clean bowl, sprinkle with flour and cover with a damp tea-towel. Leave in a warm place for around 1 hour if using warm water, or out on the worktop overnight if using cold water, to let the dough double in size and become magnificently plump.
- Punch the air out of the risen dough and turn out onto a lightly floured surface. Shape the dough into a ball, tucking the seams under, then wrap in baking paper and refrigerate for at least an hour before use.
- When ready to bake the flatbread, preheat the oven to 260°C/240°C fan/ Gas Mark 10 and sprinkle a flat baking tray with semolina to prevent any stickage.
- Place the dough on a lightly floured surface and gently massage with knuckles and fingertips outwards from the middle to form an 8 inch/20cm round. Carefully lift the dough by the edges and turn like a steering wheel, letting the weight of the dough stretch the round into a 12 inch/30cm base.
- Lay the base flat on the baking tray and dollop with your preferred quantity of lemon curd. Spread from the centre, leaving an untouched halo of dough around the edge for the crust, then sprinkle on the coconut. Dust the rim with a skiff of icing sugar to crisp the crust while baking.
- Bake for 6–8 minutes, until the crust starts to caramelise and the coconut gently toasts. Use a pizza cutter to slice and garnish with mint leaves.

Follow the recipe for the base, then top with tomato purée, herbs, mozzarella and veggies to recreate an authentic Italian pizza.

CHEESE AND CHIVE
SCONE WHEEL

Ireland's lush green pastures ensure that the local dairy is second to none. Those loyal full-bellied Friesians have contributed to quality cheddar for centuries, and a block was always stored in Granny's larder for sandwiches, salads and spuds. Still sourced from the finest local creameries, melting cheddar is tangled throughout this savoury scone loaf, with herby flecks for an earthy kick.

SERVES 8

330g self-raising flour

1 tsp demerara sugar

½ tsp salt

70g butter

125g mature cheddar cheese

Small bunch of chives, finely chopped

1 large egg

150ml milk, plus more if needed

- Preheat the oven to 200°C/180°C fan/Gas Mark 6.
- Sift the flour into a baking bowl with the sugar and salt, then rub in the butter with your fingertips, lifting and dropping to make fine crumbs.
- Grate the cheddar into a loose rick and toss into the crumbly mixture with the chives, stirring until the green is evenly dappled throughout.
- Beat the egg and milk in a separate bowl or jug, then pour almost all of it into the baking bowl, reserving a few teaspoons for a pre-oven egg wash. If the dough looks dry, add a little more milk to give a tacky consistency. A wet dough will make fluffier scones.
- Mix thoroughly with a metal knife, then use your hands to scrape the dough out onto a lightly floured surface.
- Briefly knead the dough to smooth out any cracks, then cradle onto a baking tray and gently pat to a chunky round, about 2cm thick. Coat a sharp knife in flour and use it to slice the loaf into eight wedges. They will rise and rejoin in the oven.
- Paint the wheel with the eggy glaze and bake for 20–25 minutes, until risen with a bronzed top.
- Remove the scone wheel from the oven and leave to cool before tearing into chunky wedges.

Chuck in a speckling of chopped-up crispy bacon or sundried tomatoes to bring some saltiness to the cheese and chive combo.

VICTORIA SANDWICH

Birthdays must be celebrated with cake, and a Victoria sandwich, spread with buttercream and jam, is a classic. Sharing a slice of this traditional sponge brings the family together to remember all the faces that have been lit behind the candles, sending warm wishes from generations past.

SERVES 8–10

For the cake:

225g margarine

225g caster sugar

4 eggs

225g self-raising flour

For the filling:

50g butter, softened

½ teaspoon vanilla extract

100g icing sugar

2 tbsp strawberry jam

- Preheat the oven to 180°/160°C fan/Gas Mark 4 and grease two 7 inch/18cm cake tins, at least 2 inches/5cm deep, with a little butter, then scoop a small amount of flour into each tin and tap it around to form a light coating over the grease.
- To make the cake, use an electric mixer to cream the margarine and sugar until pale and fluffy, then beat in the eggs until well combined.
- Sift the flour and gently fold it into the mixture with a metal spoon, making sure there are no hidden pockets of flour lurking at the bottom of the bowl. Scoop the batter between the two tins and spread evenly with a butter knife.
- Bake for 35–40 minutes, until the sponges spring back when touched and a metal skewer comes out clean. Slide a blunt knife around the edges of the tins to release the cakes, then tip out onto a wire rack and leave to cool completely.
- To make the filling, cream the butter, vanilla and icing sugar until pale and fluffy.
- When the cakes are cool, spread a layer of buttercream onto one cake then plop some jam onto the other. It's best to do this on the bumpy sides, as you want to keep the neatest edges visible.
- Crown the buttercreamed layer with the second cake to finish the sandwich.

The cake's taste and texture gets even more delicious after a few days if kept in an airtight tin.

'PATRICK'S HOME' UPSIDE-DOWN CAKE

Aside from my older brother's great company, we long for his visits back to Ireland for the ritual pineapple upside-down cake that is baked in jubilation at his return. With its tropical flower-power petals of pineapple, the cake has a groovy flair, and the juices from the canned fruit burst with tang that seeps into the fluffy sponge when it gets cowped at the end.

SERVES 6–8

1 small can (220g)
   pineapple rings
7 glacé cherries
170g self-raising flour
170g margarine
170g caster sugar
3 eggs

- Preheat the oven to 180°C/160°C fan/Gas Mark 4 and lightly grease an 8 inch/20cm cake tin. Drain the juice from the pineapple and lay the rings flat on the base of the cake tin, then pop a glacé cherry into each ring.
- Sift the flour into a baking bowl, then tip in the margarine, sugar and eggs and beat with an electric mixer until a smooth batter is formed
- Gently spread the mixture over the layer of fruit, making sure each of the cherries is just submerged.
- Bake for 40–45 minutes, until the sponge is springy to the touch.
- Allow to cool for a few moments, then slide a butter knife around the circumference to loosen the cake from the tin. Place a wire cooling rack upside down on the cake tin and, using oven gloves, sandwich your hands around both, then, with a swift flick of the wrist, flip the cake upside down so that the pineapple layer beams upwards.
- Leave on the rack to cool a little before slicing and serving.

Try an apple and cinnamon alternative by using sliced rings of a cored apple tossed in 2 tbsp each of cinnamon and brown sugar. You can even dot some blackberries in place of the cherries for an autumn harvest feel.

ROCK BUNS

When I first heard of Granny's 'rock buns', I assumed it was a teasing title for a gone-wrong batch of dry, brittle scones. But don't be fooled, as the title refers only to the pebbly shape of these light and crumbly treats. Classic rock buns use dried fruit but Granny's recipe kindly favours chocolate chunks, best made by bashing a chocolate bar with a rolling pin for a joyful wonkiness.

MAKES 6–8

100g chocolate
200g self-raising flour
½ tsp salt
75g margarine
75g sugar
1 egg
1–2 tbsp water

- Preheat the oven to 220°C/200°C fan/Gas Mark 7.
- Use a rolling pin to bash a bar of chocolate into chunks then set aside.
- Sift the flour and salt together in a bowl, then rub in the margarine with your fingertips until it resembles breadcrumbs. Stir in the sugar and chocolate chunks until evenly spread through the sandy mix.
- In a separate jug, lightly beat the egg, then add to the bowl and mix to combine. If required, add the water half a tablespoon at a time until the mixture comes together into a dough.
- Divide into 6–8 even mounds. Don't worry about grooming out the bumps, as their rugged form is more authentic.
- Bake for 15–20 minutes, until the knobbly bits are starting to brown, then leave to cool slightly on a wire rack.

Rock buns are best served with a little warmth still inside, as the chocolate will provide glorious melting mouthfuls.

These fun lollipops can be made using any kind of cake. Add a few drops of peppermint extract to the buttercream and freeze in a dark chocolate shell for a Choc Pop flavour.

FROSTY POPS

Ice lollies were an absolute treasure for Granny as, in the absence of a freezer, they were only available from newsagents' on a trip out to the seaside. A favourite was the Mr Frostie lollipop, a plain stick of ice cream that was slurped the whole way from shop to sea. These cake lollipops use Granny's traditional fairy-cake recipe, packed into a crisp white shell, to pay a playful homage to the cherished frosty treat.

MAKES 12

For the cake:
165g margarine
165g caster sugar
3 eggs
165g self-raising flour
½ tsp baking powder

For the buttercream:
50g butter, softened
½ tsp vanilla extract
100g icing sugar

For the coating:
200g white chocolate,
   or candy melts for
   a purer white

- Preheat the oven to 180°C/160°C fan/Gas Mark 4 and line a 12-hole baking tin with bun cases.
- Use an electric mixer to cream the margarine and sugar until smooth, then beat in the eggs. Sift in the flour and baking powder and mix with a wooden spoon to a creamy cake batter, then scoop the mixture into the cases.
- Bake for 15–18 minutes, until just risen enough to peek out of the bun cases, then transfer to a wire rack and leave to cool completely.
- Make the buttercream by creaming the butter, vanilla and icing sugar together until pale and whippy. Tear the fairy cakes from their cases and crumble into a bowl with your hands, breaking up any large chunks.
- Dollop in the buttercream a few spoonfuls at a time and mix until a squishy vanilla dough forms. You may not need all of the buttercream so store any extra in an airtight container in the freezer for up to 2 months.
- Melt the white chocolate, or whiter candy melts, over a pot of simmering water or carefully in the microwave. Pour a few spoonfuls into individual lollipop cake moulds, using only half of the chocolate. Swirl the moulds to thinly coat the entire surface, then shove a lollipop stick into each.
- Pop the moulds into the freezer for a few minutes to set, and place the remaining white chocolate back over the simmering water on a low heat to keep it liquid.
- When set, stuff the frozen lollipop shells with the cake dough, carefully prodding around the stick, and spread the remaining white chocolate over the top to seal. Use a palette knife to scrape away any drippage, then return the moulds to the freezer to set for around 10 minutes.
- When solid, allow the lollipops to come to room temperature then snap them out of their moulds and serve on the stick!

ROLY-POLY CAKE

Roly-poly cake is a heavenly light sponge and a twirly swirl of jam packed into one fat log. It reminds me of tumbling down freshly mowed slopes in the peak of summer, full of dizzy giggles and with a grassy plumage. Slice the cake into chunky spirals and serve with a drop of cream for a scrumptious summer dessert.

SERVES 6–8

3 eggs

100g caster sugar, plus extra for rolling the cake

100g self-raising flour

2-3 tbsp strawberry jam

1 tbsp icing sugar

Try a homemade jam inside the sponge using the recipes on pages 188–194).

- Preheat the oven to 200°C/180°C fan/Gas Mark 6 and line a small Swiss roll tin (about 7 x 11 inches/18 x 28cm) with baking paper.
- Crack the eggs into a baking bowl, then tip in the sugar and whisk until thick and yoghurty. You can check if the consistency is right by sweeping the whisk through the mixture – it should hold the trail left behind for at least 10 seconds.
- Sift the flour into a separate bowl, then fold into the creamy mixture a little at a time using a metal spoon and a very light touch to preserve the airiness of the cake. Pour the batter into the prepared tin and gently rock to fill the corners evenly.
- Bake for 8–10 minutes, until just firm and springy to the touch. Avoid over-baking as this will make for a cracky rolling process later.
- While the cake is in the oven, cut a large rectangle of baking paper and sprinkle well with caster sugar. Spoon the jam into a bowl and mix briskly for a few minutes to soften.
- When the sponge is cooked, flip it out onto the sugared paper and gently peel back the baking paper lining. Use a knife to carefully score a line about 1cm in from one of the short edges, working quickly before the sponge cools. This will help you to get rolling!
- Starting at the scored short edge, begin rolling towards the opposite end, then leave the rolled cake to cool on the paper with the seam facing down to stop it unfurling.
- When the sponge is no longer hot to touch, gently unroll it and spread on the jam, then reroll, tucking and twisting to a spiral. When cool, dust over a little icing sugar and trim off each end for a neat finish.

—— Biscuits & Treats ——

FIFTEENS

Fifteens are an absolute treasure in the North of Ireland, and I felt a pang of pity when I realised that unless you're an NI native you've likely never heard of them! Their name hints at the simplicity of making them, needing only 15 of each main ingredient to make the soft, sugary delight. As a local classic, you can find them in most Northern Irish coffee shops, but Granny's recipe always tastes the best.

MAKES 15

15 digestive biscuits

15 glacé cherries

15 marshmallows

200g condensed milk

75g desiccated
   coconut

- Place the digestives in a sealed bag and bash with a rolling pin, crushing them to sand.
- Quarter most of the glacé cherries and marshmallows but leave a handful or so whole, then toss into the crushed biscuits. Pour in the condensed milk, mixing to form a sticky dough, then shape into a thick sausage with your hands.
- Sprinkle the desiccated coconut evenly over a sheet of baking paper and place the sweet sausage on top. Wrap the paper tightly around the dough, pressing and rolling until the outside is evenly pebbledashed with coconut.
- Leave in the fridge overnight to chill, then slice into chunky rounds when ready to serve.

Add your own twist by
using different biscuits,
such as chocolate wafers
or oat cookies for creative
flavour combinations.

TOP HATS

Top hats are the ultimate retro treat and a true token of the Gaelic childhood. Their colourful caps have graced birthdays and bake sales for generations, and each squashy bite is a nugget of nostalgia. A neatly stacked assortment of sweet-shop bits and bobs, they are an absurdly simple way to make leftover goodies into sensational couture confections.

MAKES 12

200g milk chocolate

12 pink or white
  marshmallows

12 Smarties

- Lay 12 bun cases out on a flat baking tray or plate. The bun cases will be strong enough to contain the chocolate without the need for a cupcake tin.
- Melt the chocolate in a heatproof bowl over a pot of simmering water, or gently in the microwave. Once it is glossy and smooth, pour heaped teaspoonfuls into each bun case (1–2 tsp, depending on how thick you want your chocolate base), leaving a small amount in the bowl for adding the Smarties later.
- Gently wiggle a marshmallow into place in the centre of the chocolate puddle. Traditionally, the bigger end of the marshmallow faces down (though arguably they would look more like a top hat the other way round).
- Carefully graze one side of each Smartie against the back of a chocolate-coated spoon and add the jewel on top of each marshmallow.
- Leave the tray of top hats in a cool place for at least 1 hour until the chocolate has set: then they are ready to be scoffed.

Mix up the chocolate by melting white, milk or dark, or top the marshmallows with jellies or fruits.

LEMON COCONUT SLICES

Before the days of exotic holidays, this blend of coconut and lemon was the closest taste of the tropical. The traybake can be sliced into dainty squares of buttercup-yellow that capture the sweetness of the summer season.

MAKES 16–20

For the pastry:

75g butter

150g plain flour

3–4 tbsp water

For the topping:

50g margarine

100g caster sugar

2 eggs

100g coconut

2 tbsp lemon curd
   (page 194)

- Preheat the oven to 200°C/180°C fan/Gas Mark 4 and line a baking tray (about 7 x 11 inches/18 x 28cm) with baking paper.
- To make the pastry, rub the butter into the flour until it resembles breadcrumbs, then add the water, mixing with a knife until a dough is formed. Wrap the dough in baking paper and place in the fridge to chill while you prepare the topping.
- For the topping, cream the margarine and sugar with an electric mixer until fluffy. Beat the eggs in a separate bowl, then add to the mixture and beat until smooth. Switch to a wooden spoon to stir in the coconut until the mixture is softly scrambled.
- Take the dough out of the fridge and roll it out onto a lightly floured surface to a rectangle about ½cm thick, then use it to line the baking tray.
- Dollop on the lemon curd and spread evenly, then smother on the final coconut layer and give the tray a shake to help it settle evenly.
- Bake in the oven for 20–25 minutes, then cover with baking paper and bake for a further 15 minutes, until the coconut has lightly toasted.
- Allow the tray to cool completely before slicing into zesty bite-sized squares.

Treat yourself to
an extra slice!

YELLA'MAN

As the song goes, yella'man (or yellowman, formally) is traditionally found at the Oul' Lammas Fair, a quaint summer market that takes place every year in the coastal town of Ballycastle. Granny and Granda would have taken the whole family with ha'pennies ready to purchase a pouch of this iconic yellow treat, which is something between toffee, honeycomb and souvenir rock. Try it and see what you think!

SERVES 8–10

10g butter, plus extra
    for greasing
200g brown sugar
225g golden syrup
1 tbsp white wine
    vinegar
½ tbsp baking soda

- Lightly grease a 7 inch/18cm square cake tin with a little butter.
- Melt 10g butter in a saucepan over a medium heat. Choose a saucepan with very tall sides to prevent the boiled sweet bubbling up over the edges later.
- Tip in the sugar, syrup and vinegar and stir until all of the sugar has dissolved.
- When the ingredients have fully melted, turn up the heat and boil rapidly, with only a very occasional stir to make sure the mixture isn't sticking to the bottom of the pan. Continue boiling until the golden goo has thickened and tiny bubbles cover the surface.
- To test if the right temperature has been reached, place one droplet in a glass of cold water. If the droplet becomes brittle then the ideal 'hard crack' temperature has been reached and the yella'man is ready. Alternatively, boil until the temperature reaches 145°C on a sugar thermometer.
- Remove from the heat and leave to cool for a couple of minutes, then use a long-handled wooden spoon to stir the baking soda in quickly. The mixture will froth up furiously so take care!
- Pour the seething liquid into the prepared tin and leave to cool, gently nudging any curling edges down with a knife. When fully hardened, smash the amber toffee into wonky nuggets to serve.

Blitz the yella'man to a coarse sand and use as a crunchy topping for ice cream.

COCONUT ICE SLICE

Coconut ice was always found at summer fêtes, a pretty stack of candyfloss pink that excited the kids as they longingly awaited the school's-out bell. The flavour isn't fruity, as the colour may suggest – instead it has a cool coconut sweetness, complemented by the buttery crunch of the biscuit base.

MAKES 16–20

100g butter
200g digestive biscuits
250g icing sugar
120g desiccated
    coconut
200g condensed milk
1 tsp vanilla extract
A few drops of pink
    food colouring
Flour, to coat hands

- Line a baking tray (about 7 x 11 inches/18 x 28cm) with baking paper.
- Heat the butter in a saucepan over a medium heat until fully melted.
- Crush the digestive biscuits to a fine dust then pour in the melted butter and mix until the crumbs start to stick together. Push the biscuit mixture into the bottom of the prepared tin, packing the crumbs tightly into the base, and pop into the fridge to firm up.
- In a large baking bowl, sift the icing sugar, then stir in the coconut.
- Carve out a well in the middle and pour in the condensed milk and vanilla extract. Mix thoroughly with a wooden spoon and bring together with well-floured hands.
- Scrape half of the sticky mixture on top of the golden biscuit base and use a potato masher to press to a level layer. Coating the potato masher in flour will stop it sticking.
- Dribble a few drops of pink food colouring into the remaining coconut mixture, mixing well with a wooden spoon until rosy.
- Press the final layer of pink into the tin, heating the potato masher if needed to help smooth the top.
- Refrigerate for 4–5 hours, until fully set, then leave at room temperature for 15 minutes before slicing into squares.

Mix up the flavours and colours to any combination you like. Try a ginger-biscuit base with orange-coloured coconut or dark-chocolate biccies on the bottom with a mint-green topping.

BLAEBERRY PUDDING

Blaeberries (or 'bilberries') are wild, slightly smaller blueberries that grow in the heath on higher ground and usually ripen around Blaeberry Sunday, the last Sunday in July. When we go blaeberry picking, we usually get soaked by the rain and stained magenta with the juices, but it's all part of the craic. If you can't find bilberries or don't fancy getting your hands dirty, then regular blueberries will do fine.

SERVES 8–10

For the fruit:
450g bilberries or
    blueberries, washed
    with stalks removed
25g caster sugar

For the pudding:
100g caster sugar
150g butter, softened
2 eggs
250g self-raising flour
4 tbsp milk

- Preheat the oven to 180°C/160°C fan/Gas Mark 4.
- To prepare the fruit, tumble the bilberries into a deep pie dish (about 8 inches/20cm) and sprinkle over the sugar.
- To make the pudding, use an electric mixer to beat the sugar into the butter until dissolved into a pale fluff. Beat the egg in a separate bowl and mix in gradually, then switch to a metal spoon to carefully fold in the flour and milk.
- Decant the batter over the sugared berries and spread evenly with the back of a spoon.
- Bake for 40–45 minutes, until the sponge springs back when touched and the berries have softened to a molten goo.
- Allow the pudding to cool slightly, then scoop out to serve.

Replace the
bilberries with
450g apples, cored
and sliced, for a
traditional Eve's
pudding recipe.

BROWN LEMONADE TART

The lemonade man was a welcome visitor to many homes in the 1960s. The chirping bottles caged in his lorry delighted the children, eager for a slug of fizzy favourites like brown lemonade. Made to disguise alcohol in the shipyards of Belfast, this ruby-rust drink is a Northern Irish classic. With its lemon taste and copper hue, a splash of brown lemonade adds a local twist to this refreshingly tangy dessert.

SERVES 10–12

190g plain flour

1 tsp cinnamon

165g brown sugar

170g butter, chilled

100g chopped pecans

500ml brown lemonade, chilled

2 litres vanilla ice cream, softened

- Preheat the oven to 190°C/170°C fan/Gas Mark 5 and line a flat baking tray with baking paper.
- Sift the flour into a bowl, then shake in the cinnamon and brown sugar. Cut the butter into cubes and rub into the mixture, then add the chopped pecans and use your hands to toss everything together to a coarse crumb. Pat the mixture loosely onto the baking tray, making a kind of crumbly base with some larger chunks.
- Bake for 10–12 minutes, until lightly scorched, then remove and leave to cool completely.
- Line a 2lb/900g loaf tin with baking paper and set in the freezer while you prepare the ice-cream filling.
- Pour the chilled lemonade and vanilla ice cream into a bowl and whisk briskly until blended. The brown lemonade will fizz up in the ice cream, making it deliciously light and frothy.
- Spread half of the ice-cream filling into the loaf tin, then dump half of the baked rubble on top and repeat, finishing with a final layer of bronze crumbs.
- Cover with tin foil and freeze for 4–6 hours, or overnight.
- Before serving, remove from the freezer and leave undisturbed to soften for around 20 minutes or so, then slice to serve.

If you can't find the traditional brown fizz in the shops, clear lemonade will work just fine. You can also switch to sparkling raspberryade or cream soda for a deeper flavour.

GOOSEBERRY AND ELDERFLOWER FOOL

Wild gooseberries grow on spiky shrubs nestled in woodlands, or they can be planted in the garden for a sure supply. Be cautious when harvesting, as their jagged teeth can nip, but it's well worth battling the briars for this summer treasure. The tart tang of these taut fruits mixed with clouds of cream is a dreamily sophisticated picnic dessert.

MAKES 4

800g gooseberries

150g caster sugar, adjusted to taste

3–4 tbsp elderflower cordial

250ml double cream

250g thick natural yoghurt

4–8 mint leaves

- Top and tail the gooseberries and place in a saucepan with the sugar and elderflower cordial. If your berries are sweeter, reduce the sugar to suit.
- Simmer for about 10 minutes, stirring occasionally, until the green globes start to burst, then remove from the heat and allow to cool completely.
- Whip the cream until it's soft and velvety but not too stiff, then roughly fold through spoonfuls of yoghurt.
- Gently squash the stewed gooseberries with a fork, leaving some larger chunks, and ripple a few spoonfuls through the creamy mixture.
- Assemble layers of fruit pulp and cream into four tall glasses and top each with a sprig of fresh mint.

Refreshing fruit fools can also be made with raspberries, bilberries or rhubarb. Serve with a golden shortbread biscuit for crunch.

PEACH PETAL FLANS

As far as resourceful baking goes, it's hard to beat a fruity flan. Making the most of a pantry staple, Granny's recipe revolutionises a tin of fruit into a glorious dessert, wasting not one drop as the syrup is used as a sauce.

MAKES 4

For the sponge:

2 eggs

50g caster sugar

50g self-raising flour

For the fruit:

1 small tin peach slices
    in syrup

25ml water

1 tsp arrowroot or
    cornflour

1 tsp sugar

- Preheat the oven to 200°C/180°C fan/Gas Mark 6 and grease four 4 inch/10cm flan tins with butter, taking care to coat all the grooves and dimples. Tip a little flour into each tin, tapping and rotating so that the full surface is lightly dusted.
- Place the eggs and sugar into a large baking bowl and whisk until thick, pale and creamy. You can check if the consistency is right by sweeping the whisk through the mixture – it should hold the trail left behind for at least 10 seconds.
- Sift the flour and gently fold into the mixture using a metal spoon, taking care not to knock the air out. Divide the mixture evenly between the flan tins.
- Bake for 12–15 minutes until springy and golden brown, then remove from the oven and leave to firm up in the tins for a few moments before turning out onto a wire rack.
- While the sponges cool, sieve the peaches and catch 100ml syrup in a measuring jug then add 25ml cold water. Pour the diluted syrup into a saucepan and add the arrowroot or cornflour and sugar. Bring to a boil while stirring constantly, then reduce to a medium heat and continue stirring until the liquid bubbles clear.
- Arrange the peaches prettily into the well of each sponge and coat with the syrupy gloss. Serve with freshly whipped cream or Greek yoghurt.

Any kind of tinned fruit
can be used in this recipe.
Try mandarin oranges,
strawberries or pears.

'ALL IN ONE' RASPBERRY PUDDING

My sister Niámh is renowned for baking the best sponges with the least effort. Her 'all in one' method of throwing everything into the bowl makes light work of whipping up the fluffiest sponge so that baking this impressive dessert is a doddle. Don't worry if you get some drippage when tipping the pudding upside down – it will only add to the temptation of all that garnet goodness.

SERVES 6–8

For the fruit:
50g butter
250g raspberries
100g caster sugar

For the cake:
150g butter, softened
150g caster sugar
3 eggs
200g self-raising flour

- Preheat the oven to 190°C/170°C fan/Gas Mark 5.
- To prepare the fruit, melt the butter in a saucepan then chuck in the raspberries and sugar and allow to heat until just starting to soften.
- Pour the fruity mixture into the bottom of an ovenproof flan dish (about 9 inches/23cm round).
- To make the pudding, beat the butter, sugar, eggs and flour with an electric mixer until deliciously thick and creamy. Layer the mixture over the fruit until all traces of raspberry are submerged.
- Bake in the oven for 40–45 minutes, until the sponge springs back when touched.
- Allow to stand for a few minutes, then press an upside-down plate tightly against the top of the dish and give the cake a deft flip upside down. Carefully slip off the dish to reveal the mountain of raspberry lava on top.

Raspberry pudding is best enjoyed while still warm and oozing.

AUTUMN

There's a welcome cosiness about autumn's invite to stay indoors,
peeling off soggy socks and soothing sniffles with warm spices
and belly-filling breads. Nature is flogging all its goods before its
winter snooze, advertising a rich harvest of blackberries, nuts and
apples – not just for dunking. Granny gathered these flavours
for her Halloween spread, flickering under the squiggly whizz of
fireworks, and saved any extras for lunchbox treats. These recipes
honour the mellow maturity of autumn and make a good excuse
to retreat to the comfort of the stove.

BANANA BREAD

The scent of this bread alone is enough to warrant its baking. The familiarity of banana mingled with sweet cinnamon notes is a deliciously warm greeting after being soaked to the skin in an autumn shower. Tuck into a warm slice or two and curl up with a good book to indulge in a bit of guiltless hibernation.

SERVES 8–10

100g butter

150g sugar

2 eggs

2 large ripe bananas (overripe bananas are best because of their sweetness)

1 tsp vanilla extract

100ml milk

1 tsp baking soda

1 tsp salt

1 tsp cinnamon, plus extra for dusting

250g self-raising flour, plus extra for dusting

- Preheat the oven to 180°C/160°C fan/Gas Mark 4 and line a 2lb/900g loaf tin with baking paper.
- Place the butter in a saucepan and melt over a low heat, then leave to cool for a few minutes.
- In a baking bowl, use an electric mixer to whisk together the sugar and melted butter, then add the eggs and mix well. Make sure the butter isn't too hot or it might cook the eggs.
- Mash the bananas with a fork, then add to the baking bowl along with the vanilla and milk and continue mixing to a lumpy, bumpy goo.
- Mix in the baking soda, salt and cinnamon, then switch to a wooden spoon and stir in the flour until just combined. Pour the mixture into the lined loaf tin and dust lightly with cinnamon.
- Bake for 55–60 minutes, until the loaf rises up and turns a deep bronze.
- To check if the bread is ready, dip a skewer into its centre. It will come out clean when cooked through.
- Use the baking paper to lift the banana bread out of the tin and place on a wire rack to cool.

Exploit the classic combination of banana and peanut butter by cutting into slices and spreading on a thick layer of crunchy or smooth.

BARMBRACK

Granny's stove always held a teapot, brimming with a dark musky liquid that was so strong she'd say it would stick to your ribs! The warm flavours of the ritual Irish cuppa are delicately infused into this recipe, bringing a tea-toned comfort to the bread.

SERVES 8–10

250g sultanas

55g glacé cherries

75g soft brown sugar

2 tsp cinnamon

1 tsp mixed spice

150ml cold tea

150g self-raising flour

1 egg

- Start the process the day before by tipping the fruit, sugar, cinnamon and mixed spice into a bowl. Pour in the cold tea, then cover and leave to soak overnight.
- The next day, preheat the oven to 180°C/160°C fan/Gas Mark 3 and line a 2lb/900g loaf tin with baking paper.
- Mix the flour into the infused fruit mixture. Make a well with a wooden spoon, then beat the egg in a cup and mix into the bowl until well combined. Spoon the batter into the lined loaf tin and pop a few extra cherries on the top.
- Bake for 55–60 minutes, until a skewer comes out clean. If the loaf is browning too much on top, cover it with baking paper then return it to the oven.
- Remove the brack from the oven and allow to sit for a few moments before slipping it from the loaf tin onto a wire rack to cool.

Replace 50ml of the tea with whiskey for the grown-up version!

TREACLE BREAD

Treacle's deep flavour is an old favourite. The inky syrup is savagely sweet and gives a dark colour to this rustic bread. A few sticky spoonfuls make a comforting, rich loaf – perfect when searching for solace in the bread tin.

SERVES 10–12

325ml buttermilk

3 tbsp treacle

250g plain flour

250g wholemeal
    bread flour

2 tsp baking soda

1 tsp salt

- Preheat the oven to 220°C/200°C fan/Gas Mark 7.
- Submerge a metal spoon in boiling water to heat up, which will allow it to glide through the dark, sticky treacle a bit easier.
- Warm the buttermilk in a small saucepan over a low heat, then spoon in the treacle, stirring until smooth.
- Mix the flours, baking soda and salt in a bowl with a wooden spoon.
- Gradually add the warmed liquid from the saucepan, stirring well until a soft dough forms. If the dough seems too dry, add a splash more buttermilk to loosen.
- Turn the dough out onto a floured surface and shape into a round, then use a knife to score with a cross about 1cm deep.
- Bake for 35–40 minutes, until risen and darker on top.
- When fully cooled, tear into quarters and slice to serve.

Toast the treacle bread and top with crispy bacon for a sweet and salty weekend brunch.

FARMHOUSE WHOLEMEAL COB

This rustic brown bread has an inviting warm glow and a crust that's speckled like farmyard hens. It's a real feast for the senses, from the earthy scent to the hail of crackling seeds. Slice the loaf for hearty sandwiches to brighten up lunchboxes when September strikes.

SERVES 8–10

350ml tepid water

7g sachet fast-action dried yeast

250g strong white bread flour

250g wholemeal bread flour

1 tsp salt

1 tsp brown sugar

80g mixed seeds, plus extra for the top

2 tbsp extra virgin olive oil

- Place the tepid water (about the temperature of your hand) and yeast into a bowl and leave for around 8 minutes, until the water turns cloudy.
- Meanwhile, sift the white flour into a large baking bowl and add the wholemeal bread flour, salt, sugar and seeds. Nudge a well into the centre of the flour and pour in the yeast liquid and the oil, then mix to form a soft dough.
- Tip the dough out onto a lightly floured surface and use the heel of your hand to knead for at least 8 minutes, until it can be stretched to a thin veil without tearing. Alternatively, use a mixer with a dough hook. Place the dough back into the bowl and cover with a damp tea-towel, then leave in a warm place to rise for 1½–2 hours, until doubled in size.
- Tip the risen dough out onto a lightly floured surface and give it a punch to knock out the air. Knead briefly and mould into a smooth, tight round by pulling the edges in and tucking any seams into the middle of the bread.
- Shovel a generous handful of mixed seeds over a damp tea-towel and gently turn the bread top down onto it. Lift the corners of the tea-towel and cradle the bread for a few moments to help bind the seeds to the top for a crunchy crust.
- Line a flat baking tray with baking paper and set the dough on it seed-side up, then carefully cover with a tea-towel and leave on the worktop to prove for a further 45 minutes, until doubled in size.
- Preheat the oven to 220°C/200°C fan/Gas Mark 7.
- Bake for 30–35 minutes until lightly golden, then remove the loaf from the baking tray and bake on the oven shelf for a further 5–10 minutes, until the bottom sounds hollow when tapped.
- Remove from the oven and place on a wire rack to cool before slicing.

Stuff slices with
salad, meat and
cheese for a hearty
wholegrain lunch.

HARVEST TEA BREAD

A drink of tea is almost too wet without a slice of something to soak it up. This neat little loaf is the tastiest choice for a tea-break snack, stuffed full of chunky fruit and nuts that capture the flavours of an autumn harvest.

SERVES 8–10

100g butter

80g caster sugar

2 medium eggs

1 tbsp honey, plus
   extra for glazing

225g self-raising flour

¼ tsp salt

1 tsp cinnamon,
   plus extra for dusting

1 medium apple

50g chopped walnuts

- Preheat the oven to 180°C/160°C/Gas Mark 4 and line a 2lb/900g loaf tin with baking paper.
- Use an electric mixer to blend the butter and sugar until creamy. Beat the eggs and honey in a jug and stir gradually into the mixture until well combined. Sift in the flour, salt and cinnamon and fold into the mixture with a wooden spoon until just combined.
- Cut an apple into quarters and peel 3 of the pieces, then chop into rough, chunky nuggets. Save one section with the peel still on to use for decoration later. Slide the chopped apple and walnuts into the baking bowl and stir evenly through the mixture, then scrape into the loaf tin.
- Thinly slice the remaining apple quarter, and arrange neatly down the middle of the loaf, finishing with a skiff of cinnamon on top.
- Bake for 55–60 minutes, then reduce the heat to 170°C/150°C/Gas Mark 3 and continue to cook until bronze on top and firm to touch.
- Remove from the tin and leave on a wire rack to cool.
- Brush the loaf with a little honey and slice to serve.

Granny Smiths are a great apple for this recipe, as their tartness cuts through the sweet loaf.

Cakes & Buns

CARROT CAKE

This is my daddy's absolute favourite! Perhaps it's the deceptively virtuous mention of veg in the title that earns his health-conscious seal of approval, or the vivid flecks of carrot. Despite the garden veggies, there's no denying the decadence of this cake, with its moist, sweet spices and creamy icing.

SERVES 10–12

For the cake:

225ml vegetable, sunflower or rapeseed oil

4 eggs

225g light muscovado sugar

225g self-raising flour

1 tsp cinnamon

½ tsp ground ginger

½ tsp mixed spice

1 tsp baking soda

225g carrots, peeled and coarsely grated

100g walnuts, finely chopped

1 lemon, zest and juice

For the topping:

225g cream cheese

3 tsp lemon juice

150g icing sugar

6–8 whole walnuts

- Preheat the oven to 170°C/150°C fan/Gas Mark 3 and lightly grease an 8 inch/20cm round cake tin.
- Pour the oil, eggs and sugar into a bowl and whisk either by hand or with an electric mixer until smooth. Sift in the flour, spices and baking soda and mix with a wooden spoon to combine into a batter.
- Fold the grated carrots into the mixture with the chopped walnuts, lemon zest and juice, reserving 3 tsp juice for the icing. Scrape the mixture into the tin and shake lightly to an even spread.
- Bake in the oven for 55–65 minutes, until a skewer comes out clean.
- Gently loosen from the tin with a blunt knife and transfer onto a wire rack until cold, then horizontally slice the cake to make two even layers.
- For the icing, beat together the cream cheese, reserved lemon juice and icing sugar until soft and creamy.
- Spread half onto one side of the cake and cap with the second layer.
- Swirl the rest of the icing on top and garnish with a handful of walnuts.

Lightly toasting the nuts for 10 minutes in a hot oven will boost their flavour and fill the kitchen with a glorious scent.

SCHOOL-DINNER SPONGE

Fluffy sponge with jam and coconut is a canteen classic. It's a nostalgic reminder of bygone school days, as the lunch ladies came round with the jug of custard, topping-up the dishes of their secret favourites to make them 'big and strong'. Usually it was wolfed down in a race for the playground, so make the most of slowing down to enjoy a scrumptious slice or two.

SERVES 9

For the sponge:

115g butter, softened

115g caster sugar

2 eggs

150g self-raising flour

1 tsp baking powder

1 tsp vanilla extract

2–4 tbsp milk

For the topping:

5–6 tbsp raspberry jam, seedless for a smoother topping

75g desiccated coconut

For the custard:

2 tbsp custard powder

425ml milk

2 tsp sugar

Squeeze a splodge of red food colouring into the custard to make it just like the classic 'school-dinner' pink.

- Preheat the oven to 180°C/160°C/Gas Mark 4 and line a 9 inch/23cm square tin with baking paper.
- To make the sponge, beat the butter and sugar until pale and creamy. Crack the eggs into a separate bowl, beat, then whisk into the mixture a little at a time. Sift the flour and baking powder and fold in with the vanilla extract.
- Mix in the milk a tablespoon at a time, until the mixture just drops off the spoon. Pour into the prepared tin, scraping the walls of the bowl clean with a spatula.
- Bake for 30–35 minutes until risen up and golden on the top, then remove from the oven and allow the cake to cool slightly in the tin for about 10 minutes.
- Dollop the jam onto the sponge while it still has some heat in it, as this will make spreading it much easier, then dust over a shower of coconut.
- Use the baking paper to lift the cake from the tin, then slice evenly into neat cubes and transfer each onto a cooling rack.
- To make the custard, pour a little of the milk into a jug and mix in the custard powder until all the lumps are gone.
- Pour the remaining milk and the sugar into a saucepan and bring to the boil, then add it to the jug and stir to combine. Tip the sauce back into the saucepan and heat while stirring until thick and creamy.
- Plate up the jammy sponge topped with a liberal drizzling of custard.

ORLAGH'S CHOCOLATE CAKE

Chocolate cake is no-nonsense deliciousness. My sister Orlagh requests this as her birthday cake every year, placed perfectly in September when the dense, dark chocolateness is needed to cushion the sore end of summer. Welcome in the darker nights with this rich, decadent dessert that is sure to quench your cravings for something sweet.

SERVES 8–10

For the cake:

165g margarine

165g light brown sugar

3 eggs

135g self-raising flour

1 tsp baking powder

40g cocoa, plus extra for dusting

2 tbsp boiling water

1½ tsp instant coffee

2 tbsp warm milk

For the topping:

150g butter, softened, plus extra for greasing

300g icing sugar

150g chocolate-hazelnut spread

- Preheat the oven to 180°C/160°C fan/Gas Mark 4 and grease a 7 inch/18cm cake tin with a blob of soft butter, then tip in a pinch of cocoa powder and tap the tin while rotating it to coat the inside.
- Use an electric mixer or wooden spoon to cream the margarine and sugar until smooth and paler in colour. Beat the eggs in a separate bowl then mix into the creamed mixture. Sift the flour, baking powder and cocoa powder and use a metal spoon or spatula to fold thoroughly into the mixture, making sure that no pockets of powder escape the mixing.
- Measure out the boiling water and stir in the coffee until fully dissolved, then heat the milk and pour into the mini espresso. Swirl the liquids to blend and splash into the bowl, mixing to combine to a soft batter.
- Pour the batter into the prepared tin and level with the back of a spoon.
- Bake for 35–40 minutes, until risen and a metal skewer comes out clean from the centre. Keep a careful eye on the cake, as over-baking will make it dry.
- Remove from the tin and transfer to a wire rack to cool completely.
- To make the topping, beat the butter and icing sugar together with a wooden spoon or electric mixer until pale.
- Spoon in the chocolate-hazelnut spread and mix thoroughly to a rich, silky buttercream. When the cake is cool, slather a thick layer of the nutty chocolate cream on top.

Bejewel the cake with
fresh raspberries on top
for a fresh pop of colour.

APPLE AND CINNAMON MUFFINS

These muffins pack mouthfuls of rich harvest flavours. They are wonderfully easy to whip up on a cosy kitchen-bound afternoon, safe from blustery storms. Enjoy them hot, torn from their cases and drowned in creamy custard, or on the go as a snack.

MAKES 12

300g self-raising flour

3 tsp cinnamon

150g margarine

150g demerara sugar

3 apples

2 eggs

A little milk, as needed

- Preheat the oven to 220°C/200°C fan/Gas Mark 7 and line a 12-hole tin with muffin cases.
- Sift the flour and cinnamon into a bowl then rub in the margarine with your fingertips.
- Add the sugar and stir well, until evenly mixed through.
- Peel and chop the apples into small bites then add to the bowl, or grate them in if you desire a less chunky texture.
- Beat the eggs in a cup, then stir into the mixture with a wooden spoon.
- If the mixture looks too thick, add a little milk a teaspoon at a time to make a dropping consistency.
- Divide the mixture evenly between the muffin cases.
- Bake for 15–18 minutes, until golden brown and firm to the touch.
- Tip from the tin and place on a wire rack to cool.

Steal one straight from the muffin tray when no one is looking.

COCONUT SQUARES

The hairy face and 'ooooing' expression of a coconut gives a ghostly vibe to the Halloween spread. It's gorgeously refreshing just chopped into chunks, but it brings a deep creamy flavour to this tasty traybake. Marry it with an elegant lick of dark chocolate and chewy dried fruits for an irresistible bittersweet fusion.

MAKES 16–20

200g plain chocolate

100g butter

200g caster sugar

2 eggs

200g desiccated coconut

100g dried mango, chopped

100g dried cranberries

- Preheat the oven to 180°C/160°C fan/Gas Mark 4 and line a baking tray (about 7 x 11 inches/18 x 28cm) with baking paper.
- Melt the chocolate over a bowl of gently simmering water, or cautiously in the microwave, then pour it in an even layer onto the baking tray. Put the tray into the fridge or freezer to set while you move on to the top layer.
- Beat the butter and sugar together until light and fluffy, then beat in the eggs until well combined. Add the coconut and dried fruit to the bowl and stir until they are spread evenly through the mixture.
- Spoon the coconut mixture evenly over the set chocolate.
- Bake for 25 minutes, then cover the top with baking paper and return to the oven for a further 10–15 minutes until browned on top.
- Allow to cool, then pop the tray back into the fridge for a few hours until the chocolate has solidified.
- When fully set, cut the traybake into squares to serve.

This recipe is a simple
solution for gluten-free
baking! You can also swap
cranberries and mango for
cherries, sultanas or dried
apricots if you prefer.

CHOCOLATE CHIP COOKIES

Getting the knack for perfect cookies can be tricky. Too soft and they will spread like giant puddles in the oven; too stiff and the cookies will be dry and brittle. With the days drawing to an early close, autumn is a great time for plenty of practice, so you can master irresistibly soft and chewy cookies in no time.

MAKES 12

100g bar of chocolate
   of choice
110g butter, softened
100g brown sugar
75g caster sugar
1 tsp vanilla extract
1 egg
165g self-raising flour
½ tsp baking powder
½ tsp baking soda
Pinch of salt

- Use a large kitchen knife to roughly chop the chocolate into chunky morsels, then set aside.
- With an electric mixer, mix the butter, both sugars and vanilla together for just a few moments, then beat in the egg. Sift the flour into the bowl along with the baking powder, baking soda and salt, then stir with a wooden spoon until only just combined. Overmixing will toughen the dough. Tumble in the fragmented chocolate, and quickly mix through evenly.
- Bring the dough together into a ball, then wrap in baking paper and leave in the fridge to chill for around 1 hour.
- Preheat the oven to 180°C/160°C/Gas Mark 4, and line a flat baking tray with baking paper.
- When the dough has chilled, use a spoon or ice-cream scoop to portion out 12 balls and space evenly on the baking tray.
- Bake for 10 minutes, until puffy domes rise in the middle.
- Remove from the oven and lightly lift and drop the baking tray on the worktop to deflate the puffiness and give them a rugged crackle on top. Return the tray to the oven and cook for a further 5 minutes, until the rims are golden.
- Allow the cookies to rest on the tray for a few minutes to firm up, then move to a wire rack to cool.

After chilling the dough, try baking just one cookie to test if the dough is ready. If it spreads out too much, return the dough to the fridge for another 20 minutes or so.

THE NEIGHBOUR'S NUTTY BARS

Sharing a bite with neighbours was the done thing in Granny's day. Welcoming doorways bred stories, laughs and nuggets of baking brilliance like these nutty bars, handed to the family from a dear neighbour. They're a kind of budget Florentine, only simpler to make and tastier, as the condensed milk and crunchy cereal bring to mind the breakfast delight of cornflakes, milk and sugar.

MAKES 16–20

200g milk chocolate

200g salted peanuts

100g cornflakes

100g sultanas

200g condensed milk

- Preheat the oven to 170°C/150°C fan/Gas Mark 3.
- Line a baking tray (about 7 x 11 inches/18 x 28cm) with baking paper.
- Melt the chocolate over a pan of gently simmering water, or cautiously in the microwave, then pour it in an even layer onto the baking tray and place in the fridge to set.
- Meanwhile, put the peanuts in a sealed bag and crush with a rolling pin – aim for gravel rather than sand. Tip into a bowl along with the cornflakes and sultanas and mix until the dried fruit speckles equally throughout.
- Add the condensed milk and mix thoroughly to combine all ingredients.
- When the chocolate has hardened completely, spatter the mixture on top and spread evenly.
- Bake for 10–15 minutes, until the nuts catch a golden glow, then remove from the oven and set aside to cool.
- Place the tray into the fridge for a few hours until the chocolate has solidified.
- When fully set, cut the traybake into squares to serve.

This recipe uses about half a tin of condensed milk. Store the other half in the fridge for up to three weeks, or use it to make a delicious batch of Fifteens (see page 80).

DATE CRUMBLE SLICES

Granny used to buy dates in a big block, which I'm guessing was easier to slice up for sandwiches and curtailed snackers from pinching a few! We use Medjool dates for this traybake, as their flesh is sticky enough to bind a mound of oaty crumble and makes it succulently sweet without needing heaps of sugar.

MAKES 16–20

For the filling:
375g Medjool dates
125ml cold water

For the crumble:
130g plain flour
180g rolled porridge
  oats
Pinch of salt
½ tsp baking soda
½ tsp cinnamon
100g light brown sugar
225g butter, chilled

- Preheat the oven to 200°C/180°C/Gas Mark 6 and line a 9 inch/23cm square tin with baking paper.
- Cut the dates in half and discard the stones, then put the flesh into a saucepan and pour in the water. Stew the fruit over a medium heat until it has soaked up all the water, then lightly mash together.
- In a baking bowl, place the flour and porridge oats, then add a pinch of salt and the baking soda. Sprinkle in the cinnamon, then tip in the sugar and stir with a wooden spoon until evenly mixed. Rub in the chilled butter using your fingertips to make coarse crumbs.
- Scoop two-thirds of the crumble mixture into the bottom of the prepared tin, patting together to make a biscuity lining.
- Dollop the date filling into the tin and spread evenly with a spatula, then sprinkle the remaining third of the crumble mixture on top.
- Bake for to 45–50 minutes, or until the crumbly topping is golden, then leave to cool completely before slicing to allow the dates to firm up.

Adapt this recipe by using stewed apples or rhubarb as the filling.

CARAMEL SHORTBREAD

Friends were always welcome at Granny's quaint farmhouse, spoiled with a spread of
chocolatey treats and jovially warned that if they were hungry it was their own fault.
This buttery shortbread smothered in rich caramel and chocolate is a luxurious goodie,
so don't be surprised if your company stays for another slice!

MAKES 16–20

For the shortbread:
225g self-raising flour
55g caster sugar
170g butter

For the topping:
115g butter
115g light brown sugar
115g golden syrup
397g tin of condensed
    milk
300g chocolate

- Preheat the oven to 180°C/160°C/Gas Mark 4 and line a baking tray (about 7 x 11 inches/18 x 28cm) with baking paper.
- To make the shortbread base, sift the flour into a baking bowl and stir in the sugar. Rub in the butter with your fingertips to form breadcrumbs, then use the heel of your hand to bring together into a dough.
- Dot clumps of dough along the base of the baking tray and press to cover evenly. You can use a small drinking glass as a mini rolling pin to help smooth the surface. Pierce all over with a fork, then place a sheet of baking paper over the dough and pour on a packet of dried peas.
- Bake blind for 20–25 minutes, then remove the dried peas and bake for a further 5 minutes, until pale gold. Remove from the oven and leave in the tin to cool a little while preparing the caramel.
- Place the butter, brown sugar, golden syrup and condensed milk into a heavy-based saucepan and heat gently while stirring until the butter has melted and the sugar has dissolved completely.
- Turn up the heat to bring the caramel to a boil, then allow it to bubble until it forms a thick goo and darkens to a deep caramel colour. The caramel is ready when a droplet placed in cold water beads together to a teardrop that you can lift with your fingers. Set the caramel aside to cool slightly, then flood on top of the shortbread base. Leave in the fridge to cool completely before melting the chocolate topping.
- When the caramel is set, melt the chocolate in a heatproof bowl over a pan of simmering water, or gently in the microwave, then pour on top of the caramel, using a palette knife to smooth out any ripples.
- Leave in the fridge for 30–40 minutes to fully set, then remove from the fridge and allow it to come to room temperature before slicing into chunky squares with a warm knife.

Make half the amount
of caramel and mix with
3–4 tbsp peanut butter
for a tantalising saltiness.

SPICED APPLE POCKETS

Crisp autumn days call for a hearty treat, filled with warming spiced fruits that are sure to stop the shivers. Each pocket is bursting with lush caramelised apples, wrapped up snugly in a flaky shell. Tuck into them as a sweeter breakfast on a nippy morning or as a refreshing dessert with cream.

MAKES 6

For the filling:
2 tart green apples
10g butter
½ tsp vanilla extract
1 tsp cinnamon
3–4 tbsp brown sugar
(depending on the
sweetness of your fruit)
1 tbsp cornflour

For the pastry:
500g ready-made
puff pastry

*Life is too short for
making puff pastry
from scratch.*

For the topping:
1 egg
1 tsp caster sugar
1 tsp cinnamon

Use any leftover
pastry for sausage
rolls or a savoury
pie topping.

- Preheat the oven to 200°C/180°C fan/Gas Mark 6 and line a flat baking tray with baking paper.
- Prepare the apples by peeling, coring and chopping into chunky dice.
- Melt the butter in a heavy-based saucepan then toss in the apple and cook over a medium heat for around 5 minutes until the apples have softened slightly. Add the vanilla, cinnamon and brown sugar, stirring with a wooden spoon until the apple chunks are evenly coated and their juices start to ooze. Stir in 1 tbsp cornflour to thicken the juices, then tip into a bowl and set in the fridge to cool.
- On a lightly floured surface, roll the pastry out to a large thick rectangle around ½cm deep, then use a sharp knife or pizza cutter to dissect it into 6 equal squares.
- Place the squares onto the baking tray and dollop a spoonful of the apple compote into the middle of each, taking care not to overfill.
- Brush a little water around the edges of the square to act as a glue, then gently fold to a triangular pouch around the apple filling.
- Stitch the edges tightly by pressing firmly with a fork, and cut a few small slits in the top to let any steam escape while cooking.
- Beat the egg in a cup and brush each pastry with the eggy glaze.
- Mix the sugar and cinnamon together in a bowl, then sprinkle a sandy coating over the top of each pocket for a crunchy sweetness.
- Bake for 15–20 minutes until puffed up with a golden glow.
- Transfer onto a wire rack to cool completely, then tuck in!

BLACKBERRY CHEESECAKE POTS

There's little more charming than blackberry picking. Granny's family would spend hours foraging in the hedgerows, drenched in the golden embers of September sunshine with brambles tugging at their sleeves and purple-stained fingers. Head to the countryside to pick your own blackberries or buy a fresh punnet to mix through these no-bake cheesecakes.

MAKES 6

For the base:
50g butter
150g digestive biscuits

For the topping:
100g blackberries,
   plus extra for
   decoration
1 tbsp caster sugar
1 tbsp lemon juice

For the filling:
300g cream cheese
75g icing sugar
180g Greek yoghurt
1 tsp lemon juice

- Place the butter in a saucepan and melt over a low heat.
- Use a rolling pin to crush the digestive biscuits to a fine crumb, then stir into the melted butter until it starts to stick together. Divide the biscuit mixture between 6 small glasses, pressing down to make a chunky base.
- Chuck the fruit into a heavy-based saucepan, along with the sugar and lemon juice. Bring to a simmer, gently stirring as the berries start to burst, and continue to heat until the mixture thickens slightly, then decant into a bowl to cool.
- Tip the cream cheese and icing sugar into a large baking bowl and beat with an electric mixer until smooth. Pour in the Greek yoghurt and lemon juice and beat until thick.
- Dollop the creamy filling on top of the biscuit base and spoon on the berry compote. Set the glasses in the fridge to chill for 4–6 hours.
- When ready to serve, top with a few fresh blackberries.

Don't pick blackberries after the middle of September as folklore has it that the devil comes into them! (Really, the more mature fruits can contain little grubs that blossom into flies.)

TOFFEE APPLES

Autumn nights are undeniably enchanting, glittering with fireworks and sparklers in a haze of bonfire smoke. Granny topped off these mystical evenings with plenty of homemade nibbles, complete with a tray of toffee apples after dinner that sat tilted like witches' brooms. With a shell of sweet and sticky toffee, these sugar-wrapped apples are the ultimate dessert on-the-go while you enjoy the season's fun.

MAKES 6

6 apples
50g butter
400g dark brown sugar
1 tbsp golden syrup
2 tsp vinegar

- Prepare the apples by placing them in a bowl of boiling water for 1 minute to remove any waxy coating from them. Be sure to dry them thoroughly with kitchen paper or a tea-towel to remove any moisture that might stop the toffee from sticking.
- Snap off the stalks and shove a lollipop stick or fork securely into the core of each apple.
- Line a large flat tray with baking paper and set it near the hob where you will be making the toffee.
- Pour the rest of the ingredients into a saucepan and place on a gentle heat, stirring occasionally until the sugar has completely melted.
- When all the crystals have dissolved, bring the liquid to a boil and stop stirring.
- Let the toffee bubble for 5–6 minutes, until it darkens in colour and a droplet forms a hard ball when placed into cold water. Alternatively, boil until the temperature reaches 140°C on a sugar thermometer.
- Turn the heat to low and swiftly swirl each apple in the melted gloss, taking great care, as the toffee will be extremely hot. If the toffee starts to harden, set back on a low heat to soften.
- Drip off any excess and set the apples on the baking tray to harden for about an hour before munching.

While warm, the toffee coating can be spattered with any toppings you like. Have a go at nuts, sprinkles or crushed biscuits.

Try swapping the apples
for stewed rhubarb
or plums – simply
amend the amount of
sugar according to the
sweetness of your fruit.

APPLE TART

An apple tart was the centrepiece of Granny's Halloween spread, nestled among nuts and a ghoulish carved turnip (pumpkins were much too exotic). We keep up these traditions, though we've upgraded to a pumpkin, and use homegrown Bramley apples, stewed with a drop of sugar. Traditionally, a 50-pence piece is wrapped in baking paper and buried in one lucky slice!

SERVES 6–8

For the filling:
500g cooking apples
3 tbsp water
50g caster sugar
  (adapt to suit
  the sweetness of
  your apples)

For the pastry:
100g butter, chilled
200g plain flour
4 tbsp cold water
2–3 tsp caster sugar,
  for dusting

- Preheat the oven to 220°C/200°C fan/Gas Mark 7.
- Peel, core and quarter the apples, then place them into a saucepan with the water and sugar. You may not need all of the sugar if you are using sweet apples. Stew the fruit over a low heat, until the apples start to form a syrupy slush, then set aside to cool.
- To make the pastry, rub the butter into the flour with your fingertips until the mixture resembles breadcrumbs. Add the cold water and mix with a knife to form a soft dough. Wrap the dough in baking paper and place in the fridge to chill for 15 minutes.
- Roll two-thirds of the chilled dough to ½cm thick and use this to cover a 9 inch/23cm pie dish or ovenproof plate. Spoon the cooled apple mixture into the centre, then dampen the edges of the pastry with a little water.
- Roll out the remaining dough and use it as a lid to cover the fruit, then trim off any excess around the edges with a blunt knife.
- Seal the edges by pressing with your thumbs or a fork. If sealed tightly, the juices should not burst through, but don't fret if there is a little leakage. Use a knife to cut a slit in the top of the tart to allow steam to escape in the oven.
- Bake for 15 minutes, then reduce the heat to 200°C/180°C fan/Gas Mark 6 and bake for a further 20–30 minutes, until golden brown.
- Remove from the oven and allow to cool before dusting with caster sugar, slicing and serving with a dollop of whipped cream.

CHOCOLATE CARAMEL FONDANTS

Granny's purse would have always held a few soft caramels, and they are the perfect ingredient to give these puddings a drool-worthy melted middle. As an apostle of chocolate, this is one of my favourite recipes, and it's surprisingly easy to whip up. The cocoa mounds look quite plain, but it's true bliss when you tear into their core and uncover a rich river of molten caramel.

MAKES 4

2–4 tsp cocoa powder, for dusting the tins

100g dark chocolate

100g butter, plus extra for greasing

2 eggs

2 egg yolks

90g caster sugar

100g plain flour

4 caramel sweets

Serve immediately while hot with a blob of ice cream.

- Preheat the oven to 180°C/160°C fan/Gas Mark 4.
- Prepare 4 pudding tins or ramekins by painting with a little butter, then tip some cocoa powder in each and turn while drumming the outside to coat the inners with a chocolate dusting.
- Snap the chocolate into chunks and melt in a heatproof bowl over a pot of simmering water, or carefully in the microwave. When the chocolate is melted, add the butter and mix until silky, then set aside to cool.
- In a separate bowl, whisk the eggs and extra yolks with the sugar until thick and moussey. Sift the flour and fold through thoroughly, making sure no pockets of flour remain buried. Pour the cooled chocolate into the bowl and fold in with a spatula, using long sweeping strokes to protect the airiness.
- Fill half of each pudding tin, then nestle a chewy caramel sweet into the batter and top up the rest, giving each a wiggle to level it off.
- If you are making the puddings ahead of time, refrigerate until just about ready to serve.
- Bake for 15–18 minutes, keeping a careful eye on the puddings, until each is risen and firm to the touch with a slight wobble in the middle – this will guarantee gooey lava inside!
- Remove the puddings from the oven and leave to settle for a few moments before sliding a knife around the inner edges of each tin to loosen.
- Gently capsize each dish onto a plate and slowly lift off the tins. Dive spoon-first into the dessert to reveal a cascading stream of melted caramel.

STICKY TOFFEE PUDDING

Toffee is one of those devilishly rich flavours that will let you know you've had dessert, so I like to make wee mini portions so as not to overwhelm. Keep a pot of warm toffee sauce handy so that everyone can drench as they feel fit.

SERVES 6

For the pudding:

150g Medjool dates

100ml cold water

1 tsp vanilla extract

1 tsp baking soda

150g butter, softened

150g soft light brown sugar

2 medium eggs

2 tbsp milk

175g self-raising flour

For the toffee sauce:

75g butter

150g dark muscovado sugar

150ml double cream

- Preheat the oven to 180°C/160°C fan/Gas Mark 4 and lightly grease 6 ramekins.
- Remove the stones from the dates and roughly chop into chunky segments. Place the dates in a saucepan and add the water, then bring to the boil and cook while stirring for a few minutes until the dates have softened. Mash with a fork to a pulp or use a hand blender to remove any stubborn lumps. Stir in the vanilla then add a fizzing spoonful of baking soda to the mixture and set aside to cool.
- Use an electric mixer to cream the butter and sugar together until pale and smooth, then beat in the eggs and milk. Sift the flour and fold into the mixture, then gently stir in the date purée until well blended.
- Divide the mixture evenly between the ramekins and place them on a flat baking tray, then bake for 20–25 minutes.
- Meanwhile, to make the toffee sauce, gently heat the butter and stir in the sugar until dissolved. Pour in the cream and bring to a simmer, stirring for 2–3 minutes to a thick bronze gloss that coats the back of a spoon.
- After 20–25 minutes, when each pudding is wonderfully risen and springy to the touch, remove them from the oven and slide a blunt knife around the inner edges of each ramekin to loosen the puddings.
- Tip the puddings onto serving plates and pierce a few times with a fork to make holes for the sauce to soak into.
- Smother the puddings in rich toffee sauce before tucking in.

Store any leftover toffee sauce in the fridge for up to 3 days. It can be reheated over a low heat on the stove and drizzled onto ice cream, pancakes or even porridge!

WINTER

The first glint of winter has a magical chill, bringing with
it pale skies and frosty noses. Midwinter conditions were
certainly bleak for Granny, but the food from her stove was a
tonic that kept the family cosy through bitter blasts of snow.
She was always prepared for visitors, baking until the tins
were brimming, and whipped Christmas merriment into
family traditions anchored around homemade food. These
recipes indulge in toasty treats and cheerful nibbles to add
simple but sensational flavours to the festive season.

SODA FARLS

Granny brightened wintery dawns with soda farls straight off the griddle, oozing with puddles of butter. Named 'farls', meaning 'quarter', their shape is made by cutting a circle of dough into four. Cooking these on a hot plate gives them a crisp crust around the pillowy bread inside, which is delicious fresh, fried or toasted.

MAKES 8

500g plain flour, plus extra for the griddle
2 tsp baking soda
1 tsp salt
500ml buttermilk

- Put the flour, baking soda and salt into a bowl and mix with a wooden spoon. Gradually add the buttermilk, stirring well to form a soft, sticky dough.
- Sprinkle a griddle or flat, heavy-based frying pan with plenty of flour and heat until the flour begins to brown.
- Turn the dough out onto a floured surface, divide into two and pat each one lightly to a circle about 2cm thick. Cut a cross through each round, dividing it into four equal farls or wedges.
- Carefully place the farls on the hot griddle and allow to cook for 5–6 minutes per side, until a crisp coating forms.
- Remove the farls from the griddle and stand them upright in a row to cool slightly.
- Slice each farl in half and serve with a lick of butter.

Soda farls may be Irish but they are
not bound by a single nationality.
Use them as the bread for rich French
toast or top with passata and a sprinkle
of cheddar for an Italian vibe.

HOMEMADE VEDA

Veda is a sweet malt loaf and one of Northern Ireland's most highly rated carbs. It's often sent to family across the water, as its comforting flavour is a true taste of home! This 'homemade' version is a close replica of the secret recipe guarded by local bakeries and sold in iconic yellow wrapping. If you wind up in Ulster, be sure to buy a loaf from renowned brands like Sunblest for the real McCoy!

SERVES 8–10

230ml tepid water,
  plus extra as needed

7g sachet fast-action
  dried yeast

1 tbsp olive oil

2 tbsp barley malt
  extract

1 tbsp molasses

2 tsp brown sugar

400g strong white
  bread flour

25g roasted barley
  malt flour

25g nut brown
  malt flour

1 tsp salt

1–2 tbsp milk,
  for brushing the top

Veda and cheese is
a classic snack, but
creative combinations
are also delicious.
Try ricotta and sliced
figs or sprinkle with
cinnamon and sugar.

- Place the tepid water (about the temperature of your hand) in a large baking bowl, then sprinkle in the yeast and leave for 8–10 minutes to let the yeast waken. When frothy, pour in the olive oil, barley malt extract, molasses and sugar and stir to combine to a syrupy liquid.
- Sift the flours and salt into another large baking bowl and make a well in the centre, then pour the liquid into the dry ingredients and use a wooden spoon to give it a strong stir. You can add a little more water gradually while stirring if needed to make a soft, sticky dough.
- Tip the dough out onto a lightly floured surface and use the heel of your hand to knead for 10 minutes, until silky and elastic. Alternatively, use the dough hook on a mixer for 5 minutes.
- Wipe a fine layer of oil around a bowl, then drop in the dough and cover with a damp tea-towel. Leave to prove in a warm place for 1½–2 hours, until risen and springy.
- When the bread is risen, punch the air out of it, then give it a quick knead and form into an oblong shape. Slide the dough into the tin, then cover and leave on the counter to prove for another 45 minutes.
- Preheat the oven to 200°C/180°C fan/Gas Mark 6 and line a 2lb loaf tin with baking paper. Before the bread goes into the oven, brush it with a little milk to help shade the crust.
- Bake for 30–35 minutes, until blackened on top and the bottom sounds hollow when tapped.
- Remove from the oven and place on a wire rack to cool before slicing.

WHEATEN BREAD

Winters were hard for Granny's family, often having to plod through bus-blocking drifts to make it home from school after heavy snowfalls. But they soon warmed up by the stove, numb legs wrapped in towels, while tucking into a bowl of soup and a chunk of homemade wheaten.

SERVES 8–10

350g wholemeal
     flour
75g plain flour
1 tsp salt
1 tsp baking soda
284ml buttermilk

- Preheat the oven to 200°C/180°C fan/Gas Mark 6 and line a 2lb/900g loaf tin with baking paper.
- Place the wholemeal flour into a bowl, then sift in the plain flour, salt and baking soda, swirling with a wooden spoon to an even powder
- Gradually mix in the buttermilk, stirring with a wooden spoon to form a stiff, yet sticky, dough.
- Turn the dough out onto a floured surface and lightly shape into a thick rectangle with your hands. Place the dough into the prepared loaf tin and sprinkle the top with some wholemeal flour.
- Bake for 35–40 minutes, until risen with a brown crust on top.
- To check if the bread is ready, give its bottom a tap. It will sound hollow when cooked through.
- Allow the bread to cool slightly before slicing and dunking in a bowl of soup. Alternatively, wrap the cooled loaf in baking paper and store in the cupboard for 1–2 days.

Use this bread as the base for a stylish brunch by toasting and topping with smashed avocado and a shake of salt and chilli.

CRANBERRY AND CASHEW LOAF

Cranberries are notoriously festive. Their versatile flavour works perfectly in cookies, muffins and, of course, sauces to sweeten stuffed turkey. Take these winter fruits from bird to bread by baking them into a delightfully plump loaf, twinkling with crimson jewels. The sweet, nutty flavour is perfect for Christmas morning and will make sure you wake up merry and bright!

SERVES 12–16

30g dried cranberries

20g raisins

160ml tepid water

7g sachet fast-action
   dried yeast

25g butter

80ml milk

2 tbsp honey

2 tsp vanilla extract

385g strong white
   bread flour,
   plus extra for
   dusting

1 tsp cinnamon

1 tsp salt

35g cashews,
   roughly chopped

To reheat the loaf, sprinkle with water, wrap in tin foil and place in the oven for 10 minutes.

- Soak the cranberries and raisins in a small bowl of hot water for about 5 minutes, then drain in a sieve. This will stop the fruit absorbing liquid later and drying out the bread.
- Place the tepid water (about the temperature of your hand) in a large baking bowl and add the yeast, then leave for 8–10 minutes until frothy.
- Warm the butter, milk, honey and vanilla over a gentle heat until the butter has melted. Set aside to cool to room temperature, then stir into the yeast liquid.
- Sift the flour, cinnamon and salt into the wet ingredients and stir to combine. Bring the mixture to a tacky dough by hand then evenly mix in the cranberries, raisins and cashews.
- Turn the dough out onto a lightly floured surface and knead strongly with the heel of your hand for around 8 minutes, until springy and elastic. If the dough seems too wet, gradually add a little flour until smooth.
- Swipe the dough around the bowl to wipe off any sticky bits, then pop it into the bowl, cover with a damp tea-towel and leave in a warm place for 1½–2 hours or until doubled in size. When risen, punch the dough to deflate it and turn it out onto a lightly floured surface. Shape into an oblong and score diagonally across the top with a knife.
- Sprinkle a flat baking tray with flour and place the dough in the centre.
- Cover again and leave to prove on the worktop for a further 45 minutes.
- Preheat the oven to 200°C/180°C fan/Gas Mark 6. Fill a separate tray with boiling water and place in the oven as the bread goes in to create steam. This will give the bread a crisp crust.
- Bake for 45–50 minutes, until it is risen and sounds hollow when tapped underneath. Transfer to a wire rack and allow to cool before slicing.

CHRISTMAS CAKE

Granny's Christmas fruit cake was traditionally baked on Stir Sunday, the last Sunday of November. Baking it some weeks before Christmas gives the spices time to become merrily acquainted, and the fruit will ferment to make the cake moist. Its flavour is full and decadent so a few slices with a glass of Christmas cheer make satisfying party nibbles.

SERVES 10–12

225g margarine

225g dark brown sugar

5 eggs

225g self-raising flour, plus extra for dusting

1 tsp mixed spice

1 tsp cinnamon

680g raisins

85g cherries

115g mixed peel

2 small apples, peeled and grated

- Preheat the oven to 150°C/130°C fan/Gas Mark 2 and line a deep 8 inch/20cm cake tin with baking paper.
- Use an electric mixer to cream the margarine and sugar together until light and fluffy. Beat in the eggs, then fold in the flour, mixed spice and cinnamon to form a smooth mixture.
- Tip all the fruit into a large bowl and lightly dust with a few spoonfuls of flour to stop it from sinking to the bottom of the cake, then fold evenly into the mixture. Scrape the mixture into the tin and level off with a palette knife to an even layer.
- Bake for 2½ hours initially, then lower the oven temperature to 140°C/120°C fan/Gas Mark 1.
- Check the colour of the cake, and if it is browning too much on top, cover it with baking paper then return to the oven.
- Bake for a further 1½ hours, covering with baking paper for the last 30 minutes.
- Place on a wire rack to cool, then store in a tin to mature until Christmas.

Pour a capful of brandy over
the baked cake once a week
for a sip of seasonal jollity.

MADEIRA CAKE

In our house, Madeira is affectionately titled 'Santa's cake' due to my brother, in his early youth, tactically insisting that Madeira was Santa's favourite cake and therefore must be baked on Christmas Eve. The cake may appear bland to the eye, but each slice has an angelic creaminess. Good choice, Santa.

SERVES 8–10

175g butter

175g caster sugar

1 tsp vanilla extract

3 eggs

110g plain flour

110g self-raising flour

2–3 tbsp milk

- Preheat the oven to 180°C/160°C fan/Gas Mark 4 and line a 2lb loaf tin with baking paper.
- Cream the butter, sugar and vanilla together with an electric mixer until pale and creamy, then beat in the eggs.
- Sift both flours, then gently fold into the mixture, removing any hidden flour pockets while protecting the airy texture. Mix in the milk, adding a little at a time as required to form a creamy consistency.
- Pour the mixture into the loaf tin and bake for 35–40 minutes, until the top turns amber.
- Place on a wire rack to cool slightly before tucking into a decent slice and a cup of tea.

Add 150g glacé cherries or dried fruit to the batter before baking for a bit of variety.

You can store snowballs
for 3–4 days sealed in an
airtight container to stop
them from drying out.

SNOWBALLS

Whether they're made of ice or cake, snowballs are great fun. When Daddy was growing up there was nothing better than a heavy snowfall, and the thigh-high drifts made excellent trenches for a fluffy white war. The flurry of coconut covering these cakes gives them a frosty feel that looks wonderful as part of a winter spread – just make sure no one throws them!

MAKES 6

150g self-raising flour
60g butter
60g caster sugar
1 egg
5–6 tbsp raspberry jam
100g icing sugar
2–3 tbsp cold water
80g desiccated coconut

- Preheat the oven to 180°C/160°C fan/Gas Mark 4 and line a baking tray with baking paper.
- Sift the flour into a large baking bowl, then add the butter and sugar. Rub together with your fingers until the mixture looks like breadcrumbs.
- Beat the egg in a jug and add it to the mixture a little at a time, mixing all the while with a wooden spoon, until a stiff dough forms. You can add 1 tbsp milk if the dough is too crumbly. Tip the dough onto a lightly floured work surface and bring together with floured hands.
- Chop the dough into 12 equal parts, rolling each into a ball, then arrange the dough balls on the baking tray, leaving them with some space to grow.
- Bake for 15 minutes, until lightly browned and domed in shape, then place on a wire rack to cool.
- While the cakes cool, briskly stir the raspberry jam in a bowl to loosen.
- When cool, spread the jam onto the flat sides of the domes, using it as the glue to stick the two halves together. Leave the sandwiched domes in the fridge for 5–10 minutes to firm up.
- Meanwhile, sift the icing sugar into a bowl and add the water one spoonful at a time, mixing to a gloopy white glaze that slowly runs off the spoon. If you add too much water just tip in a little more icing sugar to rebalance.
- Tip the desiccated coconut onto a plate and place it beside your icing.
- Dip each cake into the icing, swirling to coat evenly, and let any excess drip off before tossing in an outer layer of coconut.
- Set into a bun case until the icing has set in a crisp, frosty coating.

COFFEE CAKE

Just dreaming about a hot cup of coffee is enough to bring comfort on a chilly winter's day. There's something about that bitter aroma (albeit in a sweetened latte for me) that perks up the senses and pulls you in for a warm, fuzzy hug. Baked into this fluffy sponge, caffeine tingles through every mouthful for a little extra oomph to your afternoon.

SERVES 8–10

For the cake:
225g margarine
225g soft brown sugar
4 eggs
2 tsp instant coffee
    dissolved in 1 tbsp
    boiling water, cooled
225g self-raising flour
2 tsp milk

For the filling:
75g butter, softened
150g icing sugar
3 tsp instant coffee
    dissolved in 1 tbsp
    boiling water, cooled

2 tsp cocoa powder,
    for dusting

- Preheat the oven to 170°C/150°C fan/Gas Mark 3 and line two 7 inch/18cm cake tins with baking paper.
- Cream the margarine and sugar together with an electric mixer until smooth, then beat in eggs and cooled coffee until creamy. Sift the flour and fold in with a metal spoon, winkling out any flour from the bottom of the bowl, then add the milk a teaspoon at a time to make a silky batter. Divide the mixture between the two cake tins, spreading to smooth even layers with a palette knife.
- Bake for 35–40 minutes until the sponge springs back when touched.
- Slide a knife around the inside of the tins to loosen the cakes, then tip out onto a wire rack and leave to cool completely.
- To make the filling, beat the butter and icing sugar together until creamy, then mix in the dissolved coffee until the buttercream is a milky latte colour.
- When the cakes are cool, cover one with half the caffeinated buttercream and sandwich with the other cake, then spread a swirling layer of the remaining buttercream on top. Finish with a dusting of cocoa powder.

For extra taste and crunch, crush a handful of walnuts and scatter over the cake.

IRISH FUDGE

Granny delighted her family and friends with jars of handcrafted fudge at Christmas, and somehow the simple joy of receiving home-baked goods has yet to wear off! Skip the bustling shops and spend an afternoon baking these velvety squares of sweetness, then package them up with ribbons and string for a charming homemade gift.

MAKES 20–25 PIECES

450g sugar

100g butter

170g evaporated milk

130ml whole milk

1 tsp vanilla extract

1 tsp salt

- Line a 7 inch/18cm square tin with baking paper.
- Pour the sugar, butter, evaporated milk and whole milk into a heavy-based saucepan.
- Warm over a low heat, swirling the mixture together with a wooden spoon until silky, with the sugar crystals completely dissolved.
- Increase the heat to a boil, testing the mixture as soon as it starts to bubble by placing one droplet in a glass of cold water. If the droplet forms a soft ball then the fudge is ready. Alternatively, boil until the temperature reaches 115°C on a sugar thermometer.
- Remove the pan from the heat and leave to cool for around 5 minutes, then stir in the vanilla and salt and beat vigorously with a wooden spoon until thick and no longer shiny.
- Scrape the fudge into the tin and leave on the worktop to cool completely before chopping into small, bitesize cubes.

Dust the fudge with cinnamon,
ground coffee or cocoa powder
for a sophisticated finish.

FROZEN BERRY FLAPJACKS

Nutritious, oaty flapjacks make a welcome change from the Christmas stodge, especially when they are full of frosty frozen berries. Granny loaded her recipe with warm spices, honey and a handful of cornflakes, which gives a golden crunch and qualifies them as breakfast even in the eyes of a disciplined January.

MAKES 12–16

150g butter

150g honey

3 tbsp maple syrup

250g oats

2 tsp cinnamon

50g cornflakes

75g frozen mixed berries (blueberries, blackberries, raspberries, cranberries)

- Preheat the oven to 190°C/170°C fan/Gas Mark 5 and line a 7 inch/18cm square baking tin with baking paper.
- Melt the butter over a low heat with the honey and maple syrup, stirring until golden and runny. Tip the oats and cinnamon into a large baking bowl, then lightly crush in the cornflakes.
- Pour in the sweet, buttery liquid and mix with a wooden spoon until all the dry ingredients have been coated. Fold through the frozen berries so they popple evenly through the oaty mixture.
- Spoon clumps of flapjack into the baking tin and gently pat with the back of a spoon, taking care not to squish the melting berries.
- Bake in the oven for 15–20 minutes, until the oats are lightly toasted on top.
- Leave the flapjacks to cool in the tin to room temperature, then chill in the fridge for at least 1 hour before slicing to make sure they don't crumble.

Chuck in a handful of sunflower or pumpkin seeds for an extra nutritional kick.

Mix up this recipe to include your favourite festive nibbles. Try swapping cherries for dried cranberries, or replace marshmallows with salted popcorn.

ROCKY ROAD

With mallowy hills and valleys of chocolate, the rocky road is an adventure of Christmassy tastes and textures. In Granny's day the simple pleasures of fruit, chocolate and nuts would have been eaten more modestly at Christmas (a square of chocolate after dinner or a bowl of nuts by the fire) so cramming these festive flavours into one delicious chunk is the ultimate treat.

MAKES 16–20

250g dark chocolate
150g milk chocolate
175g butter
4 tbsp golden syrup
200g digestive biscuits
150g Brazil nuts
125g mini
    marshmallows
120g red glacé cherries
A sprinkle of icing
    sugar for dusting

- Line a baking tray (about 7 x 11 inches/18 x 28cm) with baking paper.
- Snap both chocolates into chunks and place in a heavy-based pan with the butter and syrup. Heat gently until the ingredients melt into a glossy liquid.
- To make the base, place the digestives in a sealed bag and lightly crush with a rolling pin, taking care to leave larger pieces to give the rocky road the occasional boulder.
- Repeat the process with the Brazil nuts, bashing to smaller chunks.
- Tip the marshmallows, cherries, nutty chunks and crushed biscuits into a baking bowl and mix with a wooden spoon.
- Scrape the melted chocolatey mixture into the biscuit scree and stir to combine. Pour the mixture into the tray and press to an even thickness.
- Place the tray in the fridge for around 2 hours until fully set.
- When hardened, remove from the tray and sift over a skiff of snowy icing sugar.

SELECTION BOX TIFFIN

Once a big part of Santa's delivery, selection boxes were pure joy! Back then, a whole host of delicious chocolate bars netted into a garish cardboard stocking really stood out against the weekly quarter-pound of Squirrel Horn sweets. The splendour of a selection box may be somewhat redundant, but its contents become something magical when stirred into a slab of luxurious tiffin.

MAKES 16–20

For the base:
200g milk chocolate
100g butter
3 tbsp golden syrup
150g digestive biscuits
200g selection box
    leftovers

For the topping:
200g milk chocolate
Handful of selection
    box leftovers (see tip)

- Line a 9 inch/23cm square baking tray with baking paper.
- To make the base, place the milk chocolate, butter and golden syrup together in a heavy-based saucepan, and melt over a very low heat to a glossy goo.
- Weigh the biscuits into a bowl, then finely crush to a golden sand with the end of a rolling pin.
- Remove the pan from the heat and stir in the biscuits.
- Add your chosen leftover treat to the mixture, and give a quick but gentle mix to avoid melting it completely. Keep back a handful of treats for decoration – and another handful for nibbling!
- Tip the mixture into the tray and spread evenly, then place in the fridge to cool.
- For the topping, melt the milk chocolate in a heatproof bowl over a pan of hot water, or carefully in the microwave, and pour over the chilled traybake.
- Finish with a scattering of your chosen confection to showcase the flavours within.

Loose sweets like Maltesers and Smarties can be thrown in as they are, but if you're using chocolate bars, chop into chunks first.

GINGERBREAD FOLK

Gingerbread isn't half as nice unless playfully shaped into festive little fellas. These biscuits have a lovely warm flavour, and the decorations are always the best bit. Dress them up with bows and buttons to bring these sweet and spicy characters to life.

MAKES 12

For the gingerbread:
350g plain flour
2 tsp ground ginger
1 tsp cinnamon
1 tsp baking soda
100g butter
175g soft brown sugar
4 tbsp golden syrup
1 egg

For the royal icing:
See page 47

- Preheat the oven to 190°C/170°C fan/Gas Mark 5 and line a baking tray with baking paper.
- Sift the flour, ginger, cinnamon and baking soda into a large baking bowl and tousle with your hands, mixing to an even powder. Rub in the butter with your fingertips, then stir in the brown sugar. Beat together the syrup and egg and add this to the bowl a little at a time, mixing until the dough comes together.
- Tip the dough onto a floured surface and knead a little until smooth, then divide into two equal pieces. Lightly roll each piece to ½cm thickness, then use a cutter to fashion little people, placing each one on a baking tray with adequate personal space.
- Bake in the oven for 12–15 minutes, until the edges start to colour.
- The biscuits will remain soft while warm so allow them to rest on the tray, then cradle to a wire rack to cool.
- Prepare the royal icing and place it into a piping bag with a thin nozzle, then carefully pipe features and frills onto your little folk.

Use the same gingerbread recipe at Christmas to create a cosy gingerbread cottage. Roll out the gingerbread dough then use a template to cut out pieces for the walls and roof and bake on flat baking trays. Royal icing and apricot jam make excellent mortar.

SHORTBREAD

Despite being traditionally Scottish, shortbread biscuits have been gathering status throughout Ireland for centuries and were one of Granny's specialties. Their buttery texture has a naughty-niceness and a skiff of sugar gives them a joyful crunch. Pair a few with a glass of milk and a carrot to fuel the midnight journey of a Christmas visitor.

MAKES 12–16

150g plain flour

50g caster sugar, plus extra for dusting

100g butter

- Preheat the oven to 170°C/150°C fan/Gas Mark 3.
- Sift the flour and sugar together into a bowl and give it a mix with your hands to an even powder.
- Rub in the butter with your fingertips, then squeeze the mixture until it binds together as a stiff dough. If the butter is cold this can take a bit of time, but don't be tempted to add any liquid.
- Tip the dough onto a floured surface and lightly roll to around 1cm thick.
- Cut out the shortbread biscuits with a festive star-shaped cutter and place on a baking tray, allowing a little space between each in case they inflate.
- Bake in the oven for 25–30 minutes, until the edges start to turn pale gold.
- The biscuits will remain soft while warm, so allow them to rest on the tray, then dust lightly with some sugar and place on a wire rack to cool and firm.

Try adding some Christmas sparkle to the biscuits by using icing, edible pearls or sprinkles.

'WOOLLY JUMPER' OAT BISCUITS

Granny was some knitter in her day. She would trail out the Aran wool in the dim light, conducting her needles in their rhythmic, bobbing dance to craft pullovers that somehow fit snugly through every hand-me-down. These biscuits are bursting with nutritious oats, giving them a coarse, rugged texture, just like those woolly jumpers!

MAKES 12

For the biscuits:

175g self-raising flour

150g oats

150g caster sugar, plus extra for dusting

150g butter

2 tbsp golden syrup

2 tbsp milk

For the decoration:

A variety of icing pens

- Preheat the oven to 180°C/160°C fan/Gas Mark 4, and line a baking tray with baking paper.
- Tip the flour, oats and sugar into a bowl and stir with a wooden spoon until evenly mixed.
- Melt the butter with the syrup and milk over a low heat.
- Pour the golden liquid into the baking bowl with the dry ingredients and give everything a stir with a wooden spoon until a coarse dough is formed.
- Tip the dough onto a lightly floured surface and roll to around 1cm thickness, then cut out the biscuits using a jumper-shaped cutter.
- Carefully transfer the biscuits onto the tray, leaving room between each one to prevent them merging in the oven.
- Bake for 10–15 minutes until teddy-bear brown.
- The biscuits will be soft coming out of the oven, so leave on the tray for a minute or so to firm up, then dust lightly with caster sugar and place on a wire rack to cool.
- Use icing pens to decorate the woolly jumpers with appropriately garish festive patterns.

For classic oatmeal biscuits, cut into circles and dip half of each one in chocolate.

To avoid the messy shaping process, simply spread the ruffle mixture in a lined baking tin and cover with the melted chocolate before chilling and slicing into bars.

RASPBERRY RUFFLES

With candy curves dressed in dark chocolate, the raspberry ruffle is hard to resist.
Their flirtatious pink core sweetly compliments a dark-chocolate shell, creating a classic
treat that tastes as good as it looks.

MAKES 16–20

1 sachet (about 12g)
    raspberry jelly crystals
250g desiccated coconut
200g condensed milk
Plenty of flour to coat
    your hands
250g dark chocolate

- Line a flat baking tray with baking paper.
- Tip the pink raspberry jelly powder into a bowl with the desiccated coconut (I like to pause here to enjoy the scent of this fairy-dust concoction).
- Stir to spread the jelly crystals evenly through the coconut strands, then pour in the condensed milk. Mix with a wooden spoon until the dry ingredients are coated and the mixture starts to clump together.
- Dip your hands into some flour in preparation for moulding. I strongly recommend having extra flour on stand-by for re-dipping to stop your hands getting overly sticky.
- Lift a small piece of the mixture and, using light fingertips, pat and roll into a bite-sized ball, then set onto the lined tray. Resist the temptation to squeeze the mixture, as it will inevitably secure itself to your fingers.
- When the pink globes are finished, melt the chocolate in a heatproof bowl over a pan of boiling water or carefully in the microwave.
- Using two spoons, nudge each ruffle gently through the chocolate to fully coat, then set back on the tray until the chocolate has set.

MINCE PIES

Mince pies are Christmas incarnate in our house. December would be a lot less jolly without their scent to accompany carols, and port is the secret to bringing out the fruity flavours. We love mince pies so much that we discussed abolishing their seasonal binding and baking them all year round. Why not?

MAKES 12

75g butter

175g plain flour

25g icing sugar, plus more for dusting

1 egg

250g sweet mincemeat with port (if you can't find this, mix a little port into regular mincemeat)

- Preheat the oven to 200°C/180°C fan/Gas Mark 6.
- In a large bowl, combine the butter and flour by rubbing with light fingertips to form crumbs, then sift in the icing sugar.
- Beat the egg in a separate bowl, then pour into the dry ingredients and mix with your hands to form a dough. Wrap the dough in baking paper and chill in the fridge for 15 minutes.
- On a lightly floured surface, roll out two-thirds of the dough until it is paper-thin (about 1–2mm if you can manage without tearing it!)
- Cut 12 medallions from the dough with a circle cutter and use to line each hole of a 12-hole shallow bun tin.
- Plop a spoon or two of the merry mincemeat into each case, filling only to about three-quarters full to avoid sticky overspills while baking.
- Roll out the remaining third of the dough, cut out small stars and place one in the centre of each pie.
- Bake for 12–15 minutes, checking regularly, as thin pastry will cook quickly.
- Remove from the oven when the stars have a golden glow and leave to cool before dusting with a flurry of icing sugar.
- Serve gently warmed with a splash of brandy cream.

If you're a big fan of pastry, cover each pie with a pastry lid, sealed at the edges with a little water and pricked on top to let out the steam.

KRISP-MAS PUDDINGS

Christmas pudding can be a divisive dessert, attracting love or hate for its dense, boozy taste. These mini mouthfuls playfully use Granny's Mars bar square recipe to fashion bite-sized pudding look-alikes that are unanimously delicious. Roll them up and drizzle with white chocolate for a Christmas pudding that you'll really want to eat!

MAKES 12

For the puddings:
270g Mars bars
120g butter
1½ tbsp golden syrup
120g Rice Krispies

For the decoration:
100g white chocolate
Candy holly

- Line a flat baking tray with baking paper.
- Chop the Mars bars and butter into small chunks and place in a heavy-based pan with the golden syrup. Be cautious not to overdo the syrup as it will toughen the caramel to the detriment of dentures.
- Melt over a gentle heat, stirring frequently to help the ingredients meld into a luxurious caramel goo. The nougat from the Mars bars will be the last to surrender to the heat, so keep stirring until all the lumps have melted. Remove the pan from the heat and tip in the Rice Krispies, then stir until evenly coated.
- Allow the mixture to cool slightly, then scoop a little out into your hands, roll into a ball and set on the baking tray.
- Repeat until all of the mixture has been rolled into fat spheres, then transfer the tray to the fridge to chill.
- Melt the white chocolate in a bowl over a pot of simmering water, or carefully in the microwave, and top each pudding with a blob, then position a sprig of candy holly neatly on top.

To use this recipe for Mars Bar Krispie squares, simply scrape the mixture into a lined tin (7 x 11 inch/18 x 28cm) in an even layer – lightly pressing with a potato masher ensures a tightly packed tin. Melt 200g milk chocolate as for the white chocolate, then pour it evenly on top of the mixture in the tin and place in the fridge to set. When the topping is firm, remove the Krispie slab from the tray and slice into squares.

TRIFLE

Christmas dining can be a handful, so having a no-bake dessert like trifle is nifty, as the layers can be made in advance and thrown together after tea. Granny cleverly used up leftover sponge cake for the bottom layer, soaked in fruity flavours and set with a jolly wobble. Trifle is traditionally assembled in a large glass bowl but you can use individual glasses for easy serving.

SERVES 4

For the jelly layer:
425ml boiling water
1 sachet (about 12g)
    strawberry jelly crystals
160g sponge fingers,
    or leftover cake
Handful of mixed
    berries (strawberries,
    raspberries,
    blueberries)

For the custard:
500ml ready-made
    custard
or
300ml milk
1 tsp vanilla extract
3 egg yolks
1 tbsp caster sugar

For the topping:
300ml double cream
Handful of mixed
    berries (strawberries,
    raspberries,
    blueberries)
1–2 tbsp granola

- Add the boiling water to the jelly crystals and stir until fully dissolved, then set aside to cool a little.
- Line the bottom of four glass dishes with a neat pile of sponge fingers or chunks of leftover cake. Scatter over a handful of berries, then flood with the cooled jelly. Leave the dishes in the fridge for several hours, or preferably overnight, to set completely.
- If you are using ready-made custard, spoon it into a thick layer on top of the set jelly.
- To make custard from scratch, warm the milk and vanilla very gently in a heavy-based saucepan then set aside for a few moments.
- Use an electric mixer to whisk the egg yolks and sugar until pale yellow and creamy. Continue whisking and, at the same time, carefully pour in the warm milk, a little at a time.
- Pass the custard through a sieve and back into the saucepan, then set over a gentle heat once more. Don't be tempted to increase the heat, as the mixture can easily burn. Keep stirring with a wooden spoon until thick and smooth. Decant the custard into a bowl to cool to room temperature, then load onto the jelly.
- For the topping, use an electric mixer to whip the double cream until light and fluffy. Don't over-whip, as the cream will turn stiff and grainy. Dollop the peaks of cream on top of the trifle, then finish with plenty of fruit and a scattering of granola for crunch.
- Don't worry if the tiers look higgledy-piggledy, as it only adds to the charm.

For a quick version, leave out the jelly and soak the sponge in the juices of tinned fruit instead.

CHOCOLATE LOG

Like in most homes, a Christmas tree lit up Granny's quaint sitting room, oozing pine scents and twinkling with a myriad of Quality Street colours. Its warmth lingered beyond the festive season, as it was chopped into logs for the fire after the viridian boughs had faded. Enjoy the magic of yuletide logs by baking this chocolate version, smothered in ganache and dusted with a sugary snowfall.

SERVES 6–8

For the ganache:
150g dark chocolate
125ml cream

For the sponge:
3 eggs
90g caster sugar
85g self-raising flour
25g cocoa powder

A little icing sugar,
   for dusting

A woodland scene
of robins and holly
will really bring
the log to life.

- For the ganache, chop the dark chocolate into tiny shards and scoop into a large baking bowl. Gently warm the cream in a saucepan, or in short bursts in the microwave, until small bubbles appear. Pour the hot cream over the chocolate and leave for 5 minutes or so until the chocolate starts melting.
- Stir the chocolate and cream with a rubber spatula until all the lumps have melted, then leave to cool at room temperature, until it is thick enough to spread.
- Preheat the oven to 200°C/180°C fan/Gas Mark 6 and line a small Swiss roll tin (7 x 11 inches/18 x 28cm) with baking paper.
- Whisk the eggs and sugar with an electric mixer until smooth and pale. You can check if the consistency is right by sweeping the whisk through the mixture – it should hold the trail left behind for at least 10 seconds.
- Sift the flour and cocoa powder into a separate bowl and gradually fold into the egg mixture using a metal spoon and a very light touch to form a thick, moussey batter. Pour the mixture into the tin, gently tilting to spread evenly.
- Bake for 8–10 minutes, until risen and springy to the touch. Time the sponge carefully, as the dark colour may make it harder to judge when it is cooked.
- Turn the sponge out onto a sheet of baking paper and peel off the lining. Use a knife to score a line about 1cm in from one of the short edges and begin rolling tightly from there.
- Keep turning until the log is securely rolled up, then leave on the paper to cool. Gently unroll and spread with a layer of the chocolate ganache.
- Reroll the log and trim at an angle for a more realistic effect, using the cut-offs to add knobbly branches.
- Slather the ganache all over the log (the more rugged the better!) and use a fork to etch wood markings into the bark.
- Use a sieve to dust a light blanket of icing-sugar snow all over the log.

JAMS

Making jam is a great way to preserve the deliciousness of fruits in season so they can be enjoyed throughout the year. Fear of the process puts a lot of people off, conjuring images of kitchens smeared in gloopy red and pink, but jam-making is fast becoming a treasured art for the crafty and health-conscious who want to know exactly what's in their sticky spreads. Granny's traditional jam recipes use seasonal flavours and simple steps to make easy work out of handcrafting pots of fruity pleasure.

Principles of Jam Making

PECTIN

For jam to set, it relies on pectin, a natural substance found in high levels in fruits like gooseberries, apples and blackcurrants. If using low-pectin fruits, you may need to add a richer fruit (like apples or lemons) or shop-bought pectin powder to help the jam set. You can also maximise pectin power by avoiding overripe produce when picking or buying fruit.

STORING

Jams keep best in glass jars, which you can easily collect and reuse. Wash out any used jars, dry them with a clean tea-towel and warm them in a very (very!) low oven so that the glass doesn't crack in the heat. Take extra care when filling the jam jars, as the molten goo can scald an unfortunate finger, and fill the jars right to the brim to allow for shrinkage when cooled. As soon as the jars are filled, place a wax cover over the jam (you can buy these in the supermarket) and leave to cool completely before sealing with a lid. Finally, dress your jar in a circle of fabric, fastened with an elastic band, and finish with a label to identify the flavour and date it was made.

TEST FOR SETTING

Use the following process to test if your jam is ready. Alternatively, you can use a sugar thermometer and boil the jam until it reaches 105°C.

1. Put a saucer in the fridge until cold.
2. Take the jam off the heat, drop a little on the cold saucer and allow it to cool, then push the jam with your fingertip.
3. If it wrinkles slightly then the jam should set and is ready for potting.
4. If not, put the jam back on the heat and boil for a minute or so more, then test again.

Low-Pectin Fruit

These low-pectin fruits need a little help to set, so apples are added to give them a pectin boost. Follow the same method for whichever recipe you fancy. Each will make around 1.5kg of jam (about 3–4 standard jars).

BLAEBERRY (BILBERRY)

1kg bilberries
250g cooking apples
650g sugar
Juice of ½ lemon
1 tsp water

'Blaeberries' or bilberries are small wild blueberries that grow on rugged high ground. They have a sweet flavour and a fuchsia blood that looks glorious in fools and puddings. Pick them in late July or early August.

BLACKBERRY

1kg blackberries
250g cooking apples
1kg sugar
Juice of ½ lemon
200ml water

The hedgerows are festooned with blackberries in autumn, their shiny globules shielded under a tangle of prickly brambles. Their brambley ink looks great in crumbles and pairs perfectly with apple or cinnamon. Pick them between August and September.

Use half of the water for the apples and pour the other half in with the blackberries and lemon juice.

- Preheat the oven to 100°C/Gas Mark 1.
- Use a colander to wash the berries in cold water and remove any little outdoorsy bits.
- Place the sugar on a baking tray in the oven for 10–15 minutes, as this will help it to dissolve later.
- Peel, core and slice the cooking apples, then add to a saucepan with the water, simmering gently to extract the juices, then set aside (the apples will increase the pectin to help set the jam).
- In another saucepan, simmer the berries with the lemon juice until soft and oozing.
- Remove from the heat and add the stewed apples and warmed sugar, stirring well until the sugar has completely dissolved, otherwise it will burn.
- Return the saucepan to the heat and boil rapidly without stirring for about 7–8 minutes.
- When the jam appears to be setting, test using the method on page 186 (it's best to test early to avoid overboiling the jam).
- If the jam is not set, keep boiling and test every minute or so. If the jam is ready, pot and leave to cool.

High-Pectin Fruit

The following recipes are for high-pectin fruits that need no extra assistance to set. Each makes around 1.5kg of jam (about 3–4 standard jars). They all use the same method, so choose your favourite flavour and off you go!

WILD HEDGEROW

250g blackberries
250g elderberries
250g crab-apples,
    peeled and cored
250g sloes
850g sugar
600ml water

Wild hedgerow jam mingles the treasures of a scour through the hedgerows, preserving the mellow sweetness of seasonal fruits into a heavenly topping for toast or muesli. You can find crab-apple trees growing in woodlands or hedgerows, and their fruit starts to appear from late summer. Look out for elderberries' crimson stalks and pick them right after the berries turn black.

GOOSEBERRY

1kg green gooseberries
1.2kg sugar
400ml water

Gooseberries are mini beachball-like berries that grow on spiky bushes in the garden. Their refreshing tartness complements mild, floral flavours, giving a sharp, juicy zing. Pick them between June and August.

BLACKCURRANT

1kg blackcurrants
1.5kg sugar
700ml water

Blackcurrants are tiny bubbles of nutritious might that grow on leafy bunches. They popple through scones and cakes with a refreshing burst of violet that promises to stain summery whites. Pick them between June and August.

DAMSON

1kg damsons
1kg sugar
75ml water

Damsons are petite, plum-like fruits that grow on hardy trees. Their tangy flesh is a little too bitter to eat raw, but when stewed into preserves, damsons make a savoury chum for cheeses and meats and add a pinch of tartness to sweet desserts. Pick them between August and October.

When stewing the damson fruit at the start of the recipe, make sure to scoop out the stones with a teaspoon.

- Preheat the oven to 100°C/Gas Mark 1.
- Place the sugar on a baking tray in the oven for 10–15 minutes to warm, as this will help it to dissolve later.
- Top and tail, as necessary, to remove any stalks and wash the fruit.
- Simmer in a large heavy-based saucepan with the water until softened.
- Add the warmed sugar to the pot and stir over a low heat to ensure it has completely dissolved, otherwise it will burn.
- Increase the heat and boil the jam rapidly without stirring for about 8–10 minutes.
- When the jam appears to be setting, test using the method on page 186 (it's best to test early to avoid overboiling the jam).
- If the jam is not set, keep boiling and test every minute or so. If the jam is ready, pot and leave to cool.

Fruits to Macerate

Macerating is the process of leaving the fruit in sugar for several hours or overnight. Sugar pulls the juices from the fruit, deepening the flavour and getting rid of excess water to help the jam set. A little planning ahead is worth it for these gloriously sweet spreads, so choose a recipe and get started. Each will make around 1.5kg of jam (about 3–4 standard jars).

RHUBARB

1kg rhubarb
1kg sugar
Juice of 1 lemon

Rhubarb is a gangly garden shrub whose tart flavour exudes sophistication. It's sharp on the tongue but sweet on the eye, and its pretty blush tones flatter desserts and gins. Cut rhubarb between March and June.

STRAWBERRY

1kg strawberries
750g sugar (for wild strawberries increase the sugar to 1kg)
Juice of 1 lemon

There is nothing like unearthing a patch of wild strawberries hidden in the banks of woodland paths. Though slight in size, wild strawberries are packed with an intense flavour, storing all of summer's sweetness in a dainty red heart. You might struggle to track down enough wild strawberries for a whole jar of jam, so commercial ones are usually best. Luckily there are loads of great pick-your-own farms popping up, where you can spend the day harvesting the delicious fresh strawberries, or you can buy a punnet from your local farmers' market. Their season is generally short, making the delightful ruby fruits all the more precious. Pick them between April and July.

- Remove any stalks and roughly chop the fruit, then add to a bowl with the sugar and lemon juice.
- Leave the fruit uncovered to macerate overnight.
- The next day, transfer the crystallised contents to a large heavy-based saucepan and stir over a low heat to ensure all the sugar has completely dissolved, otherwise it will burn.
- Increase the heat and boil the jam rapidly without stirring for about 8–10 minutes.
- When the jam appears to be setting, test using the method on page 186 (it's best to test early to avoid overboiling the jam).
- If the jam is not set, keep boiling and test every minute or so. If the jam is ready, pot and leave to cool.

Other Spreads

RASPBERRY CHIA JAM

This recipe for raspberry jam is a much healthier alternative to regular jams, as it uses no refined sugar at all. The chia seeds work wondrously to thicken the fruit and the maple syrup adds just a hint of sweetness. The best thing is it's so simple to make, so you can cook it in minutes and cool it in time for some mid-morning scones!

MAKES 450G JAM
(about 1 standard jar)

400g raspberries (fresh or frozen, but frozen can be a tad sour)

2 tbsp maple syrup or honey

2 tbsp chia seeds

- Tip the raspberries into a heavy-based saucepan and stew slowly over a low heat until the fruit is softened.
- Pour in your chosen sweet syrup and stir to combine fully.
- Sprinkle over the chia seeds and give the mixture a good stir.
- Remove the jam from the heat and pour into a jar.
- The jam will thicken when cool as the chia seeds absorb the liquid.

LEMON CURD

Homemade lemon curd is absolutely incredible, far creamier than anything in the shops. Spread it on your morning toast for a bit of zing, with its bright yellow colour and tangy taste. You can also use it for Lemon and Coconut Scones on page 62 or create the ultimate summer flatbread by using the recipe on page 66.

MAKES 450G CURD
(about 1 standard jar)

50g butter

2 small unwaxed lemons

200g caster sugar

3 eggs

- Melt the butter in a large bowl over a pot of water just shy of boiling point.
- Wash the lemons well then grate the zest finely and squeeze out the juice, adding both to the bowl of butter.
- Add the sugar, then beat the eggs separately and add to the bittersweet concoction in the bowl.
- Stir with a wooden spoon until the ingredients meld into a silky, sunshiny gloop that is thick enough to coat the back of the spoon.
- Pour into a jar and leave to cool.

Acknowledgements

Food for me is all about family, and it is to my family that I am most grateful. Firstly, thanks to Daddy, for your infectious passion for art and nature and your knack for magical storytelling. You've painted your childhood tales so vividly I can almost taste them (well, most of them!) and your commitment to giving your kids a countryside upbringing has been the biggest blessing in my life. I don't always say it or show it (in fact I might say or show the exact opposite) but I am incredibly grateful for the time, advice, wisdom and bygone knick-knacks you have given to this book. You've guided every part of my project, with infuriating (but brilliant) perfectionism, and I hope to inherit even a pinch of your creative talents. Thanks to Mummy for your absolute baking artistry. Your years of cookery experience, coupled with a teacher's eternal patience, have pushed me through that little to-do list that we thought would never end! Thank you for the dawn starts, where we rattled out dozens of traybakes or squinted at scones to find the perfect shape, and for fixing up the kitchen (and my confidence) if things didn't go to plan. Your delicious baking is full of love and goodness, and I hope I have captured some of my admiration for you in these pages. Parents, together you have given me a childhood filled with the purest joy. From illustrated birthday cakes to heart-shaped bananas on toast for Valentine's Day, your wacky and ingenious way with food and your appreciation of how it brings us together is my endless inspiration.

I would like to thank my siblings who have contributed to these memories and recipes in their own special way. Patrick, Fi and Eoin, who visited in the midst of the mayhem and helped out by being the best taste-testers. Orlagh and Barry for keeping my spirits high with granola and bringing baby Ronan over to keep us all entertained! Niamh and Ross for being there with tea, tunes, craic and cuddles to make me smile every day, and, of course, to Bramble, for accompanying me on countless 'thinking time' walks.

I owe a huge thank you to the fantastic team at The O'Brien Press, including Ivan O'Brien, Nicola Reddy, Bex Sheridan and Emma Byrne. A special word of thanks to Michael O'Brien for having faith in my project and giving me this opportunity, and to Emma Dunne. Emma, your dedication, confidence and eternal optimism has made this journey wonderfully exciting, and I couldn't imagine many other editors being so efficient and lovely in equal measures.

I'm thankful for the great local brands such as Neill's Flour, Dromona Creameries and Dale Farm, who have generously provided oodles of yummy produce and promoted my baking career on social media. A huge thank you to Alan Glover for passing on some much-needed nuggets of photography wisdom (I owe you a cupcake, or two) and to numerous other friends and family who have ate and advised along the way.

Finally, I would like to send my thanks to my Granny McLaughlin in heaven. I hope that you are looking down on me with a smile and not scowling too much over my interpretation of your treasured recipes! Without knowing it, you've shaped who I am, and for that I am truly grateful.

Index

More delicious cookbooks from

obrien.ie

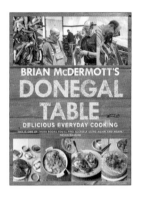